Single

Single

the Jesus model

Heather Wraight

Foreword: Clive Calver
Director General, Evangelical Alliance

Crossway Books
Leicester

ISBN 0-86584-114-6

Unless otherwise indicated, Scripture quotations used in
this book are from the Holy Bible, New International
Version. Copyright © 1973, 1978, 1984 International Bible
Society. Used by permission of Hodder and Stoughton Ltd.

Statistics quoted are from *Act on the Facts* copyright © Peter
Brierley, 1992. Published by MARC Europe. Used by
permission.

Singularly Significant Survey published on behalf of the
Evangelical Alliance in *Singularly Significant* bulletin, Issue
No. 3 1992. Used by permission.

Typeset by Avocet Typeset, 19 Church Street, Brill,
Aylesbury, Bucks.
Printed in Great Britain for Crossway Books,
38 De Montfort Street, Leicester, LE1 7GP by
Cox & Wyman Ltd, Reading, Berkshire.

Contents

Foreword

There are many aspects of the life of Jesus which provide basic sermon material. His love, cross, birth, miracles, parables and resurrection receive a great deal of attention from the church. Yet his celibacy, friendships and singleness are ignored regularly.

Family services, infant baptisms and dedications, marriages and wives groups frequently feature in church programmes. Yet singles groups are rarely found on the UK scene.

One might well be permitted to ask the reason for this apparent imbalance? After all, one-third of church attenders in Britain today are single people!

Perhaps what lies at the heart of the problem is a sense of unease. An unspoken judgment that the marital state is preferable to singleness. Yet this does not accord with the verdict of Scripture.

That is one reason for the writing of this valuable book. Heather Wraight does not seek to devalue marriage, nor does she minimize the importance of family relationships in the life of the church of Jesus Christ. Instead she simply points out the fact that single people are part of families too!

Her careful analysis of the biblical material provides a powerful corrective to the general unconscious tendency to avoid teaching on the value of singleness in the Body of Christ. We too easily forget that Jesus was a bachelor, and that Scripture values in a very special way the contribution of those who are single.

Heather and I first came to know each other when

we worked together on a group called 'Singularly Significant'. This coalition of both single and married people was called together by the Evangelical Alliance in order to challenge churches in the United Kingdom to take seriously the needs and gifts of single people within their congregations. During that time I found my own prejudices and presuppositions on this subject to be powerfully challenged. I learned how easy it is to cause pain to brothers and sisters by simply ignoring or devaluing God's path for their own lives.

Because I love being married, and enjoy my children, this does not mean that this is God's will for all his people. My views had to change, and I greatly appreciated the support and patience of those, with Heather, who served alongside me in that group. Gradually the significance of singleness dawned on me! Alongside this discovery came the realization of our need to be more inclusive of single people in church life today.

This recognition did not come from personal friendships. It arrived with a more careful exploration of biblical teaching. It is my prayer that this volume will similarly enable the reader to learn, from the teaching of Scripture, the equal value that God places on all our lives – whether we are single or married.

If you search in the pages of this book for a strident polemic on the disadvantages suffered by single people you will be disappointed. Instead the reader is offered a reasoned and conscientious biblical analysis of the subject. I found this more powerful than any human argument could ever be. It is without hesitation that I commend this book to you for both consideration and action.

There are many subjects that provoke excitement and interest among Christians today. The opportunities, difficulties and potential of singleness are rarely numbered among them. Yet this is the actual imbalance that must be redressed. This book may help many to accept the challenge – in order that singles and marrieds together may be incorporated into the life of the local church – and together demonstrate the principles of the Kingdom!

If that is the result of this volume then not only will the author be pleased, but the church of Christ blessed by the restoration of a biblical emphasis that has for far too long been ignored.

Clive Calver

Introduction

For many years I belonged to Radio Worldwide, a team of between ten and fifteen adults who make Christian radio programmes and train students in radio production. For several years I led the team, working closely together and even living semi-communally, and during that time we faced some traumatic experiences together. In one particularly difficult period of about fifteen months two of the wives died, one after a short illness and the other quite unexpectedly although she had been awaiting surgery.

I had had to come to terms with singleness for myself several years earlier, but now we had two bereaved husbands in our midst, one with three children in their teens and early twenties still living at home. Each of the team also had their own personal sense of loss to face.

In times of tragedy it is easy to withdraw into one's own emotions, yet the team had to continue to function – we had contracts with radio stations to keep and students to train! During the same period other events meant that in one way or another I was confronted with almost every form of singleness.

One of my responsibilities as leader was to plan, and most days lead, our morning prayers. I began to dig deep into the Bible to find teaching that was relevant, but I did not want only short-term answers to tide us over the immediate traumas: I wanted to find principles which would be helpful to others as well. We needed to experience 'the Father of compassion and the God of all comfort, who comforts us in all our troubles, so that we can comfort those in any trouble with the comfort we ourselves have received from God' (2 Corinthians 1:3–4).

It was that same year that I was asked to join the committee of the Evangelical Alliance's newly formed consultation on singleness, 'Singularly Significant'. I did not need reminding that singleness means much more than being unmarried! When we started to compile the study guide *Singularly Significant*, I had to look even more closely at the church's teaching on the subject.

Meanwhile I was asked to take part in seminars on singleness at Spring Harvest, resulting in quite a lot of counselling of single people; also to speak on the subject at churches and to lecture candidates for my own Mission (WEC International) on relationships for singles.

In 1990 at a conference of over one hundred of WEC's leaders from all round the world, including leaders of national churches, a resolution was passed stating: 'When teaching on marriage or relationships is given to the church, teaching on singleness should be included'. Field and church leaders commented that they agreed with the principle, but in practice, what were they supposed to teach?

This book is the outcome of my search to find biblical truth that is relevant to these diverse situations. My prime concern is not so much theological as that what we believe should work in practice on a day-to-day basis. I believe that singleness is a viable and biblical alternative to marriage. How can that be taught and modelled in our churches?

We look to the life of Jesus Christ as an example in many ways: leadership, discipling, prayer, preaching and teaching. Let us also recognize that he did not marry, and look at his life and teaching from that point of view. If the one who was 'tempted in every way, just as we are—yet was without sin' (Hebrews 4:15) could live a fulfilled single life, he can enable his followers to do the same.

My desire is that this book will be a stimulus for pastors, house group leaders and others who preach or teach. The one-third or more members of our churches who are single need to hear teaching that is relevant to their lives, not only as an occasional special series, but as an integral part of the week by week ministry.

Before going any further, I want to thank the team members of Radio Worldwide who worked with me, for their conscious and unconscious contributions to the contents of this book. Without them I would not have learned many of the lessons which made me want to write it. I am also grateful to Paul Goodliff who, as one of my pastors, challenged and encouraged me to get it done and made many helpful comments along the way.

I have quoted Scripture extensively, because busy people do not always take the time to look up references and I want the Bible to speak to you as it has to me. You may disagree with my conclusions, but please at least think about the issues!

1

Jesus' teaching on singleness

On various occasions I have asked groups to name people in the Bible who were single. They usually offer a number of suggestions including John the Baptist, Elijah, Ruth, Philip's four daughters and Jeremiah. It is often a surprisingly long time before anyone suggests Jesus. We forget or overlook that he was never married. In his life and teaching there are clues about what that meant for him, and therefore what it can mean for all Christians.

The Old Testament seems to assume that everyone would marry. There is not even a Hebrew word for bachelor, presumably because it was rarely if ever needed! For rabbis, teachers of the law, it was an unconditional duty to marry in obedience to Genesis 1:28, 'be fruitful and increase in number; fill the earth . . .'. There is some evidence that it was acceptable for a travelling rabbi not to marry, at least temporarily. However, in rabbinical writings Ben Azzai, a rabbi who was known to be celibate, was sharply criticized and accused of having been divorced and keeping it quiet, or of having an illicit sexual relationship.

In Old and New Testament times the unmarried state was misunderstood and criticized, but it was not actually forbidden anywhere in the law of Moses. Jesus did not break the law by remaining unmarried, but he did go against everyone's expectations.

Jesus was single

Jesus experienced verbal abuse, particularly from his

opponents: 'glutton', 'drunkard', 'friend of tax collectors and "sinners"' were not friendly terms. They were thrown at Jesus, or said about him on a number of occasions (Matthew 11:19 etc.). Another 'name' that was used was 'eunuch' (Matthew 19:12). It was a harsh, crude, deliberately offensive term, which Jesus is unlikely to have used if others had not already been applying it to him.

Technically, a eunuch was a man who could not have children, usually because he had been castrated, but sometimes because he had been born that way. The male servants of foreign kings and rulers were made eunuchs so that they could not interfere with the king's wives and concubines. For this reason, as well as from inferences in the Bible, it is usually assumed that both Nehemiah and Daniel, who served Persian emperors, were eunuchs.

The common caricature of such a man was that he was overweight and under-liked; he was frequently a nasty, bossy man who made the most of his senior position in court and became more and more unpleasant and despotic as he grew older. Not a nice person to know, and not a nice name to be called. 'Eunuch' could be said to be the equivalent of a four-letter word in Jesus' day; and his opponents called him that. Sex is such a powerful force in human life that both then and now it is incomprehensible to many people that Jesus chose to live without it. An illustration of this is the production in recent years of various films and books which portray Jesus as a homosexual or having an affair with Mary Magdalene.

Jesus would have been well aware that people were calling him such a derogatory name, and perhaps had a standard answer. Just once in the gospels he explained that answer to his disciples, in Matthew

19:10–12. He had been talking about divorce, a common source of argument and debate among the Jewish rabbis and teachers. As he so often did, he stated his own position clearly and unequivocally without taking sides: divorce was allowed by the law as a response to human sin and failure, not at the whim of a disgruntled husband.

The disciples' response, perhaps almost flippantly was, 'If this is the situation between a husband and wife, it is better not to marry.' I wonder what they expected Jesus to say? Probably, 'Oh, no, of course you must marry'. His answer is as surprising now as it was then; instead of saying that, he agreed with them – it may be better not to marry. What a strange and unexpected response, 'Not everyone can accept this word, but only those to whom it has been given. For some are eunuchs because they were born that way; others were made that way by men; and others have renounced marriage (or: have made themselves eunuchs) because of the kingdom of heaven. The one who can accept this should accept it.'

He was talking to a society where marriage was seen in terms of procreation. To be unable to have children was a disaster, and therefore a eunuch would almost certainly remain single. Let us look at these statements in more depth, because they have much to say about singleness. Jesus gave three reasons for being single: congenital, circumstances and choice.

Congenital singleness

'Some . . . were born that way.' There are still people with some kind of congenital handicap, either physical or genetic, which means they will never have children. In our society many of them have happy marriages. But that has not always been true, and in some parts of the world handicapped people are still denied opportunities which are open to others. In 1986 a young man came for training at Radio Worldwide from a studio making Christian programmes for broadcast on local radio in his own country. In the six months before the course he learned enough English to cope with the study, and he did really well. His government has an established training scheme for people working in the media which several others at his studio have attended. So why did this gifted young man have to come to England for training? He is from a Buddhist country, and Buddhism strives for perfection. This student had polio as a child and is now physically handicapped. He is therefore barred from receiving training in his own country, even though he is intelligent and creative. Neither did his parents expect him to find a wife, although we heard later that he had married.

Jesus did not despise people with a physical disability, rather he acknowledged that handicaps do exist, indeed at times he healed such people. Here he is not condemning the handicapped to remaining single, almost like a punishment, he simply says that physical abnormality may be one reason for not getting married. Those with a homosexual orientation would also see themselves in this category of having been 'born that way' and many who have become Christians from a homosexual background choose to remain celibate in order to keep God's law.

Single by circumstance

'Others were made that way by men'. It is rare for people nowadays to be 'made' single in the sense that

Jesus meant, though some forms of torture can have that effect. But for most people who are single, it is through no fault of their own, and they often feel they have been 'made that way by men', through the circumstances of their lives. I would put myself in this category, as would most of the single people I know.

There have been two periods in this century when many women stayed single because so many young men had been killed in one of the two World Wars. To a lesser extent that is still the case in some places in our war-torn world. However, most of those who have never married cannot blame anything so dramatic. Perhaps they just did not meet the right person. They may have had little or no opportunity because of caring for elderly parents or living in a remote area. However, when a Christian decides not to marry a non-Christian, believing that that is what the Bible teaches, the choice is limited. Many Christian women complain that there are few, if any, eligible Christian men in their church or circle of friends. Christian men who are not married by their early thirties can be put under terrific pressure to marry, after all, people say, they have plenty of choice!

Marriage is a threat to some people because of things that have happened in their lives through no fault of their own. Some do not want to marry because of problems they have encountered. Perhaps they were sexually abused as children and have an overwhelming fear of intimacy; maybe they felt rejected by parents and cannot trust relationships. These hurts need to be faced and dealt with before such people can consider the closeness of a marriage relationship.

Those who have been bereaved certainly had no

choice about becoming single, which is one of the things that makes the death of a partner so hard to come to terms with. The sense of loss can be so powerful that it is almost impossible to adjust, and indeed there are some who refuse to accept their loss, just as Queen Victoria remained in mourning for Prince Albert.

Some might say that the divorced and separated have chosen to be single, but few do so lightly. Most live through years of traumatic circumstances before coming to the fateful decision. It certainly was not a choice they ever wanted to make, or expected to when their marriage began.

Single by choice

The great majority of single people are not single by choice, but some are, and they are Jesus' third category. 'Others have renounced marriage because of the kingdom of heaven.' Jesus acknowledged a common fact in his first two categories, but here he introduced a completely new idea. It is the category he put himself in: it was more than having not married, he had actually renounced marriage. This was his explanation to his disciples and critics alike of his unusual state. He was unmarried and would remain so, not because he was physically unable to marry, nor because no one found him attractive, but because he had something more important to do with his life. The kingdom of heaven took priority for him, and to put that first he had renounced something which most people took for granted.

In Scripture Adam is seen as representative of the whole human race (e.g. Romans 5:14), whereas Christ instituted the new covenant, the kingdom of God, and is 'the firstborn among many brothers' (Romans

8:29). When God acknowledged Adam's need for companionship, he met the need by providing Eve, a wife and sexual partner. Jesus enjoyed – and therefore made possible for others – a relationship with God and his fellow beings which was complete and fulfilled without the need for marriage and a sexual partner.

Choice of attitude

However, Jesus' statement was not only a defence against his critics, it was also an invitation to others to consider that following Christ and being part of his kingdom might completely overturn their priorities too. Being a member of the kingdom of God does make demands on our lives; it requires that we 'do not conform any longer to the pattern of this world, but be transformed by the renewing of your mind' (Romans 12:2). Being a Christian means we must think differently about good and evil, change our moral standards, love our enemies, and make other radical changes in life style in line with New Testament teaching. So why should we not also re-examine our views on marriage?

I do not believe that in this statement Jesus was making out a case that a celibate life style is superior to a married one. What he was doing was presenting it as a valid alternative. What is more, it is an alternative which any single person can choose; it is not forced on them by birth or by circumstances, but is a decision which can be taken. There are people who have specifically renounced marriage in order to serve God. The example that comes to mind most readily is that of monks and nuns and it is not uncommon to find missionaries who have deliberately remained single, perhaps to go to a place where it would be unwise to take children. However, it is not necessary to have such a vocation in order to choose to remain single: for some it is the right choice while for others marriage is.

In my Mission an international conference accepted a resolution that when marriage and relationships are taught to churches, singleness should be included. How many people would have any clear idea of what to teach? The church should be challenging people to consider singleness as a possibility if they wish to make the kingdom of God a priority in their lives.

Questions

1. Do I really believe that it can be God's best for some people to remain single?

2. If I were required to teach or preach on the subject of singleness, would I have anything significant to say?

Singles do have a choice

Meanings of words change, sometimes for the worse! To say the Anglican collect about 'lovers of concord' in a church under the flight path to London's Heathrow Airport invites smiles and nudges, especially if the vicar is temporarily drowned out by a passing aircraft. Unfortunately the meaning of the word 'celibate' is changing. Until recently it meant someone who was unmarried and abstaining from sexual intercourse, often having taken a vow to remain that way for the rest of their lives. Now, however, celibacy for some people means only that they have no current sexual relationship. They have given up sex for a little while for a particular reason, perhaps to give themselves time to practise New Age-style meditation.

For centuries, Roman Catholic priests, as well as monks and nuns, have taken vows of celibacy. It is considered so acceptable and normal that if a priest gives up his calling in order to marry it can be front-page headlines in the local newspaper. The dilemma of a nun who takes a vow of chastity and then falls in love has been the plot of various films. It will certainly be front-page news if he or she has an illicit relationship which becomes known. Celibate priests – and married vicars – are just not expected to do that sort of thing, and such behaviour is frowned upon by some who would appear to have few qualms about doing the same thing themselves!

Singleness as a gift

It is strange that in Protestant churches we have come to look down on singleness. By contrast, in his teaching in Matthew 19 Jesus presented it as a valuable gift for some people: 'not everyone can accept this word, but only those to whom it has been given' (19:11). What a radical way of thinking: I can be given the gift of not being married! As with all gifts, including the gift of salvation, it must be received and entered into personally. Paul also taught that celibacy is a gift: 'I wish that all men were as I am. But each man has his own gift from God; one has this gift, another has that' (1 Corinthians 7:7). Paul told the Ephesians that gifts are not primarily for ourselves, but 'to prepare God's people for works of service, so that the body of Christ may be built up' (Ephesians 4:12). They have to be used too (Romans 12:6–8), and they all originate in the grace of God (Romans 12:6). Celibacy can be seen as one of those gifts, to be used for the benefit of others.

Many are so conditioned by the thinking of our culture that the only gift they want is the gift of a suitable husband or wife. Not having a partner around to share life is a burden, not a gift. But being celibate can be embraced as a positive gift for the sake of the kingdom of heaven.

Unconsciously many of us in the church have accepted double standards in the often unspoken assumption that someone who has no 'other half' is incomplete, even slightly odd. The words or actions of many married people, including some church leaders, imply that singles must all be desperate to find someone to marry, or marry again. If a single walks into church with a person of the opposite sex, someone will wonder when they are going to get engaged. I am not the only one who has been told at a wedding, 'Never mind, it will be your turn next.' One year the profile of me in the Spring Harvest programme included that I want to see singleness accepted by the church as a viable alternative to marriage. A couple of weeks later I was on the phone arranging some meetings when the man at the other end remarked that he thought the profile 'showed lack of faith'. His assumption was that I must be wanting a husband. I was furious, but it was a blatant example of double standards.

For single men there is the added pressure that in our culture it is still usually up to the man to start a relationship. If they choose not to, they may be accused of being selfish or homosexual.

Societies' messages to singles

Marriage is so much the norm in many non-Western cultures that it is assumed that an adult woman must have a husband somewhere. A single woman in such a culture, meeting someone she has not met before, may find herself in a conversation like this:

Stranger	How are your children?
Woman	I don't have any children.
Stranger	You don't have any children – at your age? (Pause) How is your husband?
Woman	I don't have a husband.
Stranger	Oh, when did he die?
Woman	He didn't die. I've never been married.
Stranger	Are your parents still alive?
Woman	Yes, they are well, thank you.
Stranger	Well, why have they not found you a husband?

If conversations like this occur regularly, it can be difficult to keep a balanced outlook. The whole rigmarole can become hilariously funny, which may cause offence, or it can bring up negative reactions of rejection or anger – why do I have to keep explaining myself in this way? If the woman has any lingering doubts about whether it is God's will for her to be single, they will soon surface, and may become overwhelming.

When someone becomes a Christian as a child or young person, he or she can find themselves in a very difficult position if unbelieving parents insist on marriage and there are no other Christians to marry. In one part of West Africa some young men responded to the gospel, but no young women. Who could they marry? In many societies a person is not considered an adult until they marry. In such circumstances, what should the local church or the missionary teach them?

The single missionary also comes face to face with the local attitude which he or she must understand and come to terms with to live happily in that culture. For some, such as Hindus, it is acceptable and even respectable for a man to remain single for religious reasons, although in animistic societies it may be assumed that he is a sorcerer or witch doctor. An extra pressure, more common for single men but also encountered by women, may be that local people see marriage as a means of getting to another country and so place difficulties and temptations in his or her path that never occurred at home.

These attitudes to singleness are common among ethnic minorities in pluralist societies. When people from these backgrounds respond to the gospel, singleness and marriage can be a major issue for them.

Singles included

Let us go back to Matthew 19 and look at another positive assertion for single people in Jesus' words. We are acceptable in the kingdom of heaven! That does not sound very amazing to us now, but it certainly did to his hearers, particularly with Jesus using that awful word 'eunuch'. Eunuchs were forbidden to enter the temple in the Old Testament, and therefore were excluded from worship (Deuteronomy 23:1).

We see an example of it in Nehemiah 6:10–11. The Jews' enemies were doing everything they could to stop the rebuilding of the walls of Jerusalem. They had mocked and ridiculed Nehemiah, threatened to attack the city and spread malicious rumours. Now they had a new scheme to harm Nehemiah, subversion. They hired an insider and asked him to try to persuade Nehemiah to take refuge against possible attack. The reasoning sounds so plausible, 'Let us meet in the house of God, inside the temple, and let us close the temple doors, because men are coming to kill you—by night they are coming to kill you.'

Nehemiah's reply shows that although he was the governor of the province, he was not prepared to compromise spiritually to achieve his aims, 'Should a man like me run away? Or should one like me go into the temple to save his life? I will not go!' He was not the sort of man to run away. But why would he not take refuge in the temple? Because, as a senior official of a Persian emperor he would have been a eunuch, and so it was forbidden for him. He was the leader of the people, a visionary, a tireless worker for God, but in spite of this, he was barred from the temple, forbidden to join the people in worship, excluded from the central core of his religion.

Jesus removed that barrier. Isaiah had foretold that this would happen: 'To the eunuchs who keep my Sabbaths, who choose what pleases me and hold fast to my covenant—to them I will give within my temple and its walls a memorial and a name better than sons and daughters; I will give them an everlasting name that will not be cut off' (Isaiah 56:4–5). Philip illustrated it in practice when he told the Ethiopian eunuch the good news and then baptized him (Acts 8:34–38).

Nowhere in his teaching did Jesus exclude anyone from the kingdom of heaven if they wished to enter it. And here he specifically included a category of people who were excluded by Jewish law. Most singles no longer face that kind of ostracism, though some single parents and divorcees may do, even today. But here Jesus was saying that neither a physical handicap nor our marital status affects our eligibility for the kingdom of heaven.

An alternative attitude

I believe these verses present an alternative way for those who have not specifically renounced marriage. Ask some people why they are not married and they will reply, 'Because I was never asked'. Here Jesus is saying, 'But you do have a choice'! I may not have been able to choose to marry, but I can choose my attitude towards singleness: I can continue to feel a victim of circumstances, or I can determine to accept it positively and discover what it can mean for the kingdom of heaven.

Or is putting the kingdom of God first in our lives really a choice? If I genuinely want to follow Christ wholeheartedly, it may mean some unexpected – even at first unwelcome – choices. Jesus said to his disciples, 'If anyone would come after me, he must deny himself and take up his cross daily and follow me' (Luke 9:23). Denying ourselves means different things for each of us. For some it means giving up a good job with excellent prospects of promotion and a good salary, to become a minister or vicar. For others the choice may involve leaving home, family, culture and all that is familiar to take the good news of the gospel to those who have not yet had the opportunity to hear it. Some may be asked to give financially until it hurts, perhaps forgoing a larger house or holidays abroad.

And for some it may mean deliberately and positively putting aside hopes and desires for marriage. That may not happen overnight. Soon after I joined WEC International I met and fell in love with a young man who was also expecting to join the Mission. I was certain that Radio Worldwide was where God wanted me and when my friend announced he was heading for the Far East it was hard to let him go alone. It was three or four years before I could see that decision as a positive rather than a negative one.

When God asks us to make these kind of sacrifices, he knows what he is talking about. Paul clearly tells us that in Philippians 2:6–7 or as Graham Kendrick's song puts it: 'He laid aside his majesty, gave up everything for me . . .'. We too can choose to deny ourselves and follow Jesus, to take on God's priorities, not our own. If that means renouncing marriage for the sake of the kingdom of heaven let us make it a positive choice, to be embraced wholeheartedly. 'For whoever wants to save his life will lose it, but whoever loses his life for me will save it' (Luke 9:24).

Questions

1. Have I misunderstood singleness, either for myself or others?

2. In what ways does my thinking need to change to come into line with Jesus' teaching on singleness?

3

Jesus' teaching on marriage

In the early nineties there was a popular series of adverts on British television which featured a well-known brand of coffee. Two well-dressed, obviously successful, business people lived in flats in the same house, but he ran out of coffee, and had to borrow from her. And so started a romance, with the adverts updating the story every few months, and of course always featuring a cup of coffee. Presumably sales of the coffee improved, but the adverts certainly became a talking point.

Romantic novels sell by the millions, and royal weddings are remembered with nostalgia, even though the resulting marriages may have ended so disappointingly. Weddings are the stuff of dreams, and yet for many single people they are a nightmare.

The wedding at Cana

Jesus had a very balanced view of marriage. The wedding at Cana must be preached on at thousands of weddings each year, and indeed it was a very significant time, not only because Jesus turned water into wine, but because it was his first miracle. John tells us that through this event Jesus 'revealed his glory, and his disciples put their faith in him' (John 2:11). Sometimes wedding services include words such as 'Jesus hallowed marriage by attending the wedding at Cana in Galilee'. On a number of occasions Jesus told parables about weddings, for example those about the wedding banquet and the wise and foolish virgins.

He gave a considerable amount of teaching on marriage, emphasizing the importance of a strong marriage and making bold statements such as 'what God has joined together, let man not separate' (Mark 10:9). He had challenging words to say about lust, adultery and divorce, without ever appearing aloof or unconcerned about those who faced such problems: the delicate way in which he handled the situation with the woman caught in adultery showed his compassion (John 8:2–11). People who have, as Jesus put it, 'renounced marriage' are sometimes in danger of trying to appear 'holier than thou': as though choosing to remain single is more holy than getting married. On the other hand, I have known single people who would not attend weddings because it was so hurtful to see a friend getting married when they, themselves, had no prospect of doing so. Jesus never gave the slightest glimmer of either of these attitudes: for him marriage was important, and must continue to be an integral part of human experience.

Marriage only temporary

However, in Luke 20:27–39 he gave another, and perhaps unexpected perspective: marriage is not permanent! Throughout chapter 20, Luke showed the religious leaders trying their best 'to catch Jesus in something he said so that they might hand him over to the power and authority of the governor' (verse 20). In that context a group of Sadducees came up with a question they hoped would trap him. They quoted the law of Moses about the duty a man had if his brother died, to marry the widow and have children for his dead brother. They proposed a case of a woman whose husband died before they had had a child. The man was one of seven brothers, each of whom in turn married her but died childless. After seven of them, I'm not surprised the woman died! But the crux of the story was the question, 'at the resurrection whose wife will she be?' (verse 33).

The Sadducees did not believe in the resurrection, so it was a trick question at two levels, and Jesus dealt with them both. He unequivocally put the Sadducees straight on the matter of the resurrection, and of course he was soon to demonstrate resurrection himself.

However, he did not overlook the matter of whose wife she would be. His answer makes us stop and think, 'The people of this age marry and are given in marriage. But those who are considered worthy of taking part in that age and in the resurrection from the dead will neither marry nor be given in marriage, and they can no longer die; for they are like the angels' (verses 34–36). Marriage is important for this life, but for this life only – it ends here. In heaven there will be no need for marriage, because there will be no need for procreation when we are all immortal.

A right view of marriage helps singleness

Clearly Jesus was not implying that those who were married should live as though they were not, otherwise what was the point of all his teaching on marriage? Marriage will be part of human experience until the end of the age and Jesus' return.

It is so important that it should not be entered into lightly. In an article, 'A Pastoral Strategy for Stronger Marriages', John Blatther wrote:

> One of the first things we can do to strengthen Christian marriage is to support singlehood. If

> people are to enter marriage wisely, they need to be free of inordinate pressures to escape the single state . . . We should view singlehood not as a holding pattern for the immature but as a viable option for fruitful Christian life and service. The more viable singlehood is in the church, the fewer bad choices will be made about whether and when and whom to marry.

The church's attitude to singleness and marriage is often closer to that of the world around than to biblical teaching. Society puts pressure on young people to find a boyfriend or girlfriend, and conditions them to expect to get married. A young friend of mine moved house with her parents. In a letter she wrote, 'We all like our new schools and have lots of friends, but I would ask you to pray for me, as mine is a small, mixed school, about the pressure to have a boyfriend.'

Christians' attitudes need to change so that it is OK not to have a boyfriend and indeed later, also OK not to get married. Comments from well-meaning friends like 'When are you going to settle down?' or 'Haven't you found someone yet?' show that many people's basic feeling is that singleness is unnatural and even to be pitied. Let us look biblically at singleness, to see whether it is a viable option, not second best, and so that fewer people may get married for the wrong reasons.

As well as pointing out that marriage is not permanent, Jesus made it clear that it cannot be an excuse to avoid responsibilities when he told the parable of the guests who were invited to a banquet (Luke 14:15–24). When the servant arrived to announce that it was time to come, they all began to make excuses. Three were specified, one of which was, 'I have just got married, so I can't come.' A man who had recently married was excused from military service for a year (Deuteronomy 24:5), but that is hardly parallel to refusing to go to a banquet to which you had previously been invited! There is no doubt that the parable condemned the guests who refused to come (verse 24).

I have met a number of people who told me that as a teenager they believed God wanted them in some form of full-time Christian work, but then they 'got married and settled down'! Were they wrong in their original understanding of God's plan for them or was marriage an excuse to avoid that plan? Indeed Paul pointed out that marriage can lead to divided interests making it difficult to put God first (1 Corinthians 7:32–34).

Costly discipleship

In following up this parable Jesus went further by saying that to be his disciple would be costly in terms of relationships: 'If anyone comes to me and does not hate his father and mother, his wife and children, his brothers and sisters—yes, even his own life—he cannot be my disciple' (Luke 14:26). He continued this theme in other similar verses, 'No-one who has left home or wife or brothers or parents or children for the sake of the kingdom . . .' (Luke 18:29).

What did Jesus mean when he talked about hating or leaving one's wife? Hyperbole is a common figure of speech in Hebrew and Jesus was probably overstating the case to stress the point. He can hardly have been thinking of breaking up an existing marriage, because that does not tie in with his other teaching, but the challenge to put him before all other relationships cannot be side-stepped.

C.T. Studd, the founder of WEC International, did take these words of Jesus literally, and spent many years in Africa, leaving his wife behind in London to recruit workers and deal with the administration of the Mission. That is unlikely to happen these days, nevertheless many missionary families agonize over conflicting demands of family and ministry, especially regarding children's education. Single people applying to become missionaries have to face the fact that pursuing such a calling will usually mean staying single.

Even though we may not take the words of Jesus' teaching literally, we need to take seriously the spirit behind it, that discipleship is demanding. However, we should also remember that his demands come with a promise, in this case, they will 'receive many times as much in this age and, in the age to come, eternal life' (Luke 18:30).

Paul on singleness

Paul also taught that people should get married for the right reasons when he counteracted two opposite points of view. One argument was for promiscuity: some of the Corinthians thought they could do what they liked, including their sexual activities (1 Corinthians 6:12–20). Corinth was known throughout the Greek world for the temple to the goddess Aphrodite which at one time employed one thousand female slaves as prostitutes. To those whose thinking had not changed much since they became Christians, Paul argued convincingly that our bodies belong to the Lord and we are not free to gratify our own desires, whether for food or for sex. This kind of attitude finds its parallel today: 'If it feels good, do it', and in the advice offered that the way to avoid Aids is by adopting 'safe sex' rather than abstinence.

However, some of the Corinthians had reacted strongly to such 'liberty', and gone to the other extreme of asceticism which was highly admired by some in ancient Greece. They saw sexual intercourse as unclean or unspiritual and said that a man should not marry (or should not have sexual relations with a woman: 1 Corinthians 7:1). Paul also dealt with that, although admittedly in a way that is somewhat more controversial and confusing to us. He made it quite clear that those who were married were to have a sexual relationship – but only with each other (7:2). He conceded that in some situations it was right to marry, but encouraged his readers to consider remaining single for the right reasons, not out of asceticism.

Interestingly he allowed not only for a man to remain single, but also for a woman (7:34), so giving women a choice of marital status that was quite revolutionary in that Greek setting. His motivation seems to have been that the unmarried person has more time for the things of the Lord (7:32, 34). Three phrases in chapter 7 are worth noting to show that, as always, Paul's main concern was that his readers should put God first in their lives: 'keeping God's commands is what counts' (verse 19); 'as responsible to God' (verse 24); 'that you may live in a right way in undivided devotion to the Lord' (verse 35).

As far as Paul was concerned, being an ascetic was no more acceptable than being promiscuous, and he was not in favour of either. He would have preferred people to remain single as he was (verse 8), though he did make it clear that singleness is a gift and that people have different gifts (verse 7).

The overall argument of 1 Corinthians 6 and 7 is that marriage is the normal state of affairs, but that

Christians should give serious thought as to whether it is God's plan for them. That is still valid today!

Questions

1. *For the single*: How do I view marriage? Is my priority to get married, or to know God's will? Are my reasons for wanting or not wanting to get married Scriptural ones?

2. *For the married*: How do I view singleness? Do I think of it as second best, and do I communicate that to the single people I know?

3. *For church leaders*: Are my views of singleness based on social values or biblical teaching?

4

Jesus as the bridegroom

Every country and ethnic group has its own customs
about marriage. In many, the partners are chosen for
one another by their parents; in others the man
chooses or the choice is mutual. Engagement may be
legally binding or may not exist at all. When it comes
to the actual ceremony, there is just as much variety.
Some weddings take only a few minutes, others last
all day or even a week, as we see in the Old
Testament. When King Xerxes married Esther he gave
a 'great banquet' (Esther 2:18), and as the previous
banquet had lasted seven days, we can be sure a
'great' one was longer than a few hours! When
Samson married a Philistine woman in Timnah, the
feast went on for seven days (Judges 14:12), and it
was the same when Jacob married (Genesis 29:27).

In Britain the bride and groom usually meet in a
neutral place such as a church or registry office. In
many cultures the bride is taken to the bridegroom,
but in Jesus' time it was customary for the bridegroom to come to the bride. Many names and titles
are given to Jesus and one of them is the bridegroom,
for he has come to his bride, the church.

In the Old Testament the people of Israel were
portrayed as the bride and God as the bridegroom,
'As a bridegroom rejoices over his bride, so will your
God rejoice over you' (Isaiah 62:5), and 'your Maker
is your husband' (Isaiah 54:5). Isaiah joyfully compared receiving salvation with preparing for
marriage: 'I delight greatly in the LORD; my soul
rejoices in my God. For he has clothed me with

garments of salvation and arrayed me in a robe of righteousness, as a bridegroom adorns his head like a priest, and as a bride adorns herself with her jewels' (Isaiah 61:10). In Hosea the Lord declared, 'In that day you will call me "my husband" . . . I will betroth you to me for ever . . .' (Hosea 2:16, 19). In the New Testament the picture changed slightly, with the church becoming the bride and Jesus Christ the bridegroom.

Jesus as the bridegroom

John the Baptist was the first to take up this theme and apply it to Jesus, 'I am not the Christ but am sent ahead of him. The bride belongs to the bridegroom. The friend who attends the bridegroom waits and listens for him, and is full of joy when he hears the bridegroom's voice. That joy is mine . . .' (John 3:28–29).

Jesus accepted and used the same picture when he was asked why John's disciples and the Pharisees fasted, but his disciples did not. He replied, 'How can the guests of the bridegroom fast while he is with them?' (Mark 2:19)

In the parable of the wise and foolish virgins all ten were waiting for the bridegroom. Those who were prepared and had brought enough oil for their lamps were able to go in to the wedding banquet when the bridegroom arrived, while those who had not come prepared were shut out of the celebration (Matthew 25:1–13). Later in the chapter Jesus made it clear that this parable (and the one about the talents which followed it) were warnings to be ready for when he, the Son of Man, would return in his glory. We do not know when he will come back, but when he does it will be as the bridegroom to claim his bride.

The book of Revelation uses the same analogy, 'For the wedding of the Lamb has come, and his bride has made herself ready' (Revelation 19:7). In Revelation the bride is the Holy City, the new Jerusalem (21:2), but Paul used the same imagery when 'talking about Christ and the church' in the context of his teaching on marriage (Ephesians 5:32).

The bride of Christ

I have occasionally met people who claim to be 'married to Christ', but biblical scholars see little evidence to support this for individuals. However, each of us as Christians is a member of the body of Christ, the church, and the whole church is indeed his bride. There is therefore a sense in which our relationship to him should be that of a bride with her bridegroom – certainly the Bible makes it clear that we should have a deep love for Christ which causes us to obey him, 'If you love me, you will obey what I command' (John 14:15). Jesus commanded us to, 'Love each other as I have loved you' (John 15:12). Our relationships within the body of Christ should reflect our relationship with Christ as the head and bridegroom, whatever our personal marital status.

The Bible presents some interesting puzzles for us: in this picture of the church as the bride, men as well as women are included, single as well as married. Another side of the coin, as we will see in chapter 5, is that women are heirs of God because they have been adopted as sons (Romans 8:13–17). As a woman, I used to get annoyed at being called a son of God, until I realized that male Christians are part of the bride of Christ! In Christ, both genders become something they cannot be in the natural world.

Marriage and singleness for the prophets

The teaching of the Old Testament on Israel as the bride was primarily given by Isaiah and Hosea, two prophets whose personal lives illustrated it in some way. Indeed for most of the major prophets, their personal relationships played a significant part in their ministry and message.

Isaiah was married, although we know nothing about his wife except that she also was a prophet (8:3). However, his two sons became part of his ministry. Their names had significant meanings: Shear-Jashub means 'a remnant will return' (7:3) and Maher-Shalal-Hash-Baz, 'quick to the plunder, swift to the spoil' (8:3). Isaiah was told to take Shear-Jashub with him when he went to meet King Ahaz with a message about Judah being taken into captivity (chapter 7). We know well the verse 'The Lord himself will give you a sign: The virgin will be with child and will give birth to a son, and will call him Immanuel' (Isaiah 7:14) – we hear it read most Christmases. I do not think I have ever heard it put in context: Isaiah telling King Ahaz that the king of Assyria would overthrow Israel. Standing alongside Isaiah, as evidence by his name of the truth of the message, was the son who was called 'a remnant will return'. But if that was not enough, God would send another Son who would bring about a 'return' even more significant than the return from exile.

Maher-Shalal-Hash-Baz is equally as important in his father's ministry, underlining that exile could not be avoided, because the people had rejected God (8:3–10). Again there was the reference to Immanuel, God with us (verses 8, 10). Isaiah summed it up in 8:18, 'Here am I, and the children the LORD has given me. We are signs and symbols in Israel from the LORD Almighty, who dwells on Mount Zion.'

Isaiah's children were part of his message. Jeremiah's lack of them was part of his. In Jeremiah 16:2 God said to him, 'You must not marry and have sons or daughters in this place'. God went on to explain why: the catastrophe that lay ahead would mean that those who had children would be unable to care for them. To underline the significance of this message, Jeremiah was to remain single as a living illustration of his message of judgment.

Ezekiel had to endure bereavement to emphasize the importance of his message. '"Son of man, with one blow I am about to take away from you the delight of your eyes. Yet do not lament or weep or shed any tears . . . do not mourn for the dead . . . ". So I spoke to the people in the morning, and in the evening my wife died. The next morning I did as I had been commanded' (Ezekiel 24:16–18). Ezekiel must have loved his wife dearly because God called her the delight of his eyes, and yet her death and Ezekiel's response to it were central to his message of the need to return to the Lord. I wonder what they said to each other that day, knowing that she was about to die?

Hosea lost his wife in a different way. God's message to him initially was, 'Go, take to yourself an adulterous wife and children of unfaithfulness' (Hosea 1:2). Hosea obeyed by marrying Gomer. While they were living together she had three children, probably only the first of which was Hosea's child. The meaning of their names must have had personal as well as national significance: Jezreel, the site of a massacre, Lo-Ruhamah meaning 'not loved' and Lo-Ammi, 'not my people' (1:4–9). Imagine the anguish there must have been in that family, especially when Gomer returned to her old ways: the cruel comments

43

in a small community, the ostracism of the children, the questions in Hosea's heart. Yet he was eventually told to go and buy Gomer back to illustrate the lengths to which God goes to show his love to his people (chapter 3).

We have already seen in chapter 1 that Nehemiah and Daniel were eunuchs. Both of these men were only able to have the impact they did because of the official position they held. That position necessarily meant that they had to remain single, although we read almost nothing of the personal cost involved.

So we have six major characters in the Old Testament whose personal relationships played a central part in their ministry to the people of God. We can infer that our personal relationships also contribute to our message of the Good News. Whether we are married, as Hosea and Isaiah were, single like Jeremiah, Nehemiah and Daniel, or bereaved like Ezekiel, the way we live should demonstrate the truth of what we believe. A gospel song of a few years ago said, 'What you are speaks so loud that the world can't hear what you say, They're looking at your walk, not listening to your talk, They're judging by your actions every day.' Whatever our marital status the way we live can be prophetic in the sense that it illustrates in practice the truth of what we say we believe.

Question

Do I see my personal relationships as my own business, or am I prepared to live in such a way that whether single or married, my life shows people that what I believe works?

5

Identity and independence

One of the biggest questions people ask themselves these days is 'Who am I?' There is talk about identity crises and mid-life crises, and there are popular psychology items on television and liberally scattered through the pages of women's magazines.

Meet people for the first time, and the getting-to-know-you small talk usually includes some sort of identity question: what do you do; are you married; do you know so-and-so etc.? One of the stigmas of unemployment is the implication that if I do not have a paid job I have no identity, and one of the stigmas of being single is that I do not belong to anyone.

We find our identity in all sorts of things: nationality, job, possessions, educational achievements, belonging to a club or peer group, relationships etc. That is why a move, a change of job, redundancy or retirement often uncovers any lurking sense of insecurity. 'Who do I belong to?' also has a range of answers: am I my parents' child, my children's parent, my husband's wife, my teacher's pupil, my brother's sister, my boss's employee?

Who am I?

Our self-awareness depends on relationships: if single people often feel they do not belong to anyone, it is hardly surprising that they may struggle with wondering who they are. This feeling is particularly strong when a relationship comes to an end, whether a broken engagement, a bereavement or a separation.

Sudden, perhaps unexpected singleness like this can pitch people headlong into questions and emotions which are more likely to creep up slowly on those who gradually become aware that not yet being married means they are single.

As Christians our most important relationship should be the one we have with God, so that our identity is that I am first a child of God, then a spouse, parent, child, employee, etc. We all need to discover this for ourselves to enable us to live healthy emotional lives, whether married or single. I fell into the trap of looking for identity in my work, which led to an almost obsessive perfectionism. Within four years of joining Radio Worldwide I had worked myself to a standstill and had to have three months off. Some fall into the trap of thinking that marriage will solve any identity problems. However if one or both partners is looking for all the answers to 'Who am I?' from the other partner, the resulting dependency can strangle the relationship.

If we look to Jesus as our example, we find that he knew exactly who he was, based on his relationship with his Father. We see the start of the process in the temple at Jerusalem when he was twelve years old. On that occasion he asked his worried parents (who had spent three frantic days searching for him), 'Didn't you know I had to be in my Father's house?' (Luke 2:49). When Jesus was baptized, the voice from heaven said, 'You are my Son, whom I love . . .' (Luke 3:22). God declared their unique relationship in the hearing of the crowds that day, rather than conferring on Jesus at that moment a status which he had not previously known about.

Jesus was of course the Son of God in a unique way, being totally God and yet at the same time totally human. However, we also become children of

God when we believe in Jesus and accept his gift of salvation, as John makes clear, 'to all who received him, to those who believed in his name, he gave the right to become children of God' (John 1:12). Paul deals with this in depth in his letter to the Romans chapter 8, setting out what it means to be a son of God. We are not the Son of God, but we are all sons of God, as members of his family.

In Greek culture, as in many others before and since, only sons could inherit from their father. This is why Paul called us all 'sons' whether we are male or female; the importance of being a son is that we become co-heirs with Christ in order that we may share his glory (Romans 8:14–17). One of the exciting aspects of being a Christian is that in Christ every one of us are eligible to inherit all the Father has made available for us. We too can have a father–child relationship with the Father because we have been adopted as his sons (Ephesians 1:5). What a tremendous sense of identity and belonging that can give us!

We can know the Father, as Jesus did. Philip initially found it impossible to understand this and requested Jesus to 'show us the Father and that will be enough for us' (John 14:8). Jesus' response, 'Anyone who has seen me has seen the Father' (verse 9), was not limited to Philip. We find the same concept in Matthew's gospel, 'No-one knows the Son except the Father, and no-one knows the Father except the Son and those to whom the Son chooses to reveal him' (11:27). So often our relationship with God reflects our relationships with others, rather than the other way round. The Fatherhood of God is especially important for people who do not feel that they belong to anyone, or have no one to care for them.

Why am I here?

John's gospel makes it abundantly clear that Jesus not only knew exactly who he was but also why he was here. We see this first in John 4:34–38, when the disciples could not understand Jesus' response to their offer of food, 'My food is to do the will of him who sent me and to finish his work'. The next four verses tell us what his work was: to reap a harvest. God sent Jesus to this earth to fulfil his will by accomplishing the task of redemption.

The theme of being sent for a purpose appears repeatedly in John:

> My Father is always at his work to this very day, and I, too, am working . . . He who does not honour the Son does not honour the Father, who sent him (5:17, 23).

> The very work that the Father has given me to finish, and which I am doing, testifies that the Father has sent me (5:36).

> I have come down from heaven not to do my will but to do the will of him who sent me (6:38).

> As long as it is day, we must do the work of him who sent me (9:4).

> Father . . . I said this for the benefit of the people standing here, that they may believe that you sent me (11:41, 42).

> When a man believes in me, he does not believe in me only, but in the one who sent me (12:44).

What is the reason for life?

Knowing God as our Father not only gives us an identity, but also provides a purpose which has major implications for the way we live. Amazingly, if we look at Jesus' teaching carefully, we find that we can share in various aspects of the relationship which Jesus had with his Father, especially those which were his reason for being on this earth.

Christians have always struggled with what Jesus meant when he said, 'anyone who has faith in me will do what I have been doing. He will do even greater things than these, because I am going to the Father' (John 14:12). Whatever his original meaning, we cannot escape the fact that there is a job for us to do, a purpose for our lives. Many books have been written and sermons preached to show that God has a plan for each individual, and yet so often single people seem to be waiting for marriage before they can get on with fulfilling that purpose. Jesus had no such restriction, so why should we?

His plans cover every day of our lives. Just as they do not wait until we marry to start, neither do they come to an end when a marriage does. Those who have been bereaved or divorced need time to come to terms with their loss and grief, but then they need to be encouraged that God has not wiped them out of his plans. They can still fulfil his purpose, even though their circumstances have changed radically.

Singles too can find and do the will of God for their lives. Indeed, getting on with obeying God is much more satisfying and fulfilling than waiting, in the hope that one day circumstances may change and then I may be able to do something for God.

Independence versus God's will

One of the big advantages of singleness is the freedom to make our own decisions. Yet Jesus did not have that freedom and in many senses, as Christians neither do we. We cannot live independent, self-sufficient lives, thinking only about our own wants and desires. Jesus did not live that way: he said of himself, 'the Son can do nothing by himself; he can do only what he sees his Father doing' (John 5:19). He makes it clear that the same principle is true for us, 'apart from me you can do nothing' (15:5).

Especially in the West, we cherish our independence, but there is no place for a selfish independence in the kingdom of God! One of the tests of our love for God is whether we obey him (14:15). Even Jesus had to come to a crucial decision as to whether he would fulfil God's will. In the Garden of Gethsemane he was in tremendous anguish, yet he still said, 'Father, if you are willing, take this cup from me; yet not my will, but yours be done' (Luke 22:42). Every time we pray the Lord's Prayer, we say, 'Your will be done on earth as it is in heaven'. One of the questions Christians ought to ask is, 'Am I prepared to be the answer to my own prayer, and allow God's will to be done in my life?'

Obeying God and working to fulfil his will is not a negative, restricting thing which leaves life poorer. One of the consequences of obedience is that, 'my Father will love him, and we will come to him and make our home with him' (John 14:23). Wow! Once this becomes a reality in our lives it not only puts independence into perspective, it also takes precedence over all other relationships. Discovering this in my own life made an enormous difference, but having lived closely with other team members over many years, I have seen that it is as important a lesson for married people as it is for singles. As well as loving him, Jesus commands us to love one another. We will return to that theme in a later chapter.

Resources

God gives us his resources in order to fulfil his purpose. Jesus was sent by God as we saw earlier, but then so are we. 'As the Father has sent me, I am sending you', he said to the frightened disciples after the resurrection (John 20:21). Then he breathed on them and said, 'Receive the Holy Spirit' (verse 22). That was an essential prerequisite for accomplishing his purpose: 'you will receive power when the Holy Spirit comes on you; and you will be my witnesses in Jerusalem, and in all Judea and Samaria, and to the ends of the earth' (Acts 1:8). Nowhere in Scripture is being a witness limited by age, sex, marital status or anything else.

'Who am I?', 'Why am I here?', 'What's the purpose of life?' are important questions. Jesus had no problem in answering them; let us find our answers in him rather than looking for them in other relationships.

Questions

1. How would I describe who I am, as distinct from what I do?

2. Does my identity depend on another person, or is someone dependent on me? How can I or they find our own identity in Christ?

3. Am I consciously fulfilling God's will for my life, or am I waiting for my circumstances to change before thinking about it?

6

Family

In Britain more and more people live on their own. There are two distinct groups: those who have been married but who are now on their own, mostly divorcees or older people, and those who have not married, including more and more young people who have chosen to live alone who in the past would not have left home until they got married. In 1961 only 12 per cent of households consisted of one person but by 1990 it was 26 per cent. This accounted for more than one in ten of the population and the number continues to rise.

Over the same period the proportion of people living in 'traditional' families – father, mother and dependent children – dropped from 52 per cent to 41 per cent while the number of single-parent families rose to over 1 million by 1990.

These trends are not limited to Britain; throughout the world the meaning and significance of family life is changing. What does 'family' mean for single people? Is it an irrelevant or hurtful word, or can Christians invest it with new meaning as well as emphasizing its traditional meanings?

The family at Nazareth

What did 'family' mean to Jesus? We have already seen that his teaching underlined the importance of marriage, but it is interesting to look at his own family life. There is no doubt that Jesus' human parents were special people, who were trusted by

God for their unique role. They gave Jesus a good home where he learned and developed towards maturity. After the incident at Jerusalem when he was twelve, we are told, 'he went down to Nazareth with them and was obedient to them . . . Jesus grew in wisdom and stature, and in favour with God and men' (Luke 2:51–52). He learned how to relate to people. In the gospels we never see him unwittingly breaking social conventions. We find that he can quote the Old Testament extensively, and he could read – when he visited the synagogue at Nazareth he looked for and read a specific section of Isaiah (Luke 4:17–19). He learned his father's trade too, and presumably was good at it, as he never did anything badly or half-heartedly!

No family is perfect

However, all was not necessarily easy for him. It is commonly assumed that Joseph died at some point before Jesus took up his public ministry. This is inferred from various places where we read of Mary, or his mother and brothers, and the fact that when Jesus was dying he asked John to take care of his mother (John 19:26, 27). This would have been unnecessary if Joseph were still alive.

Jesus was the oldest son, and so when his human father died he would not only have had to cope with his own loss, but also become head of the family, support his mother and help care for his younger brothers and sisters (Mark 6:3). This was all part of 'sharing in our humanity' (Hebrews 2:14), which means he knows what it is like when we face similar circumstances. It would be fascinating if some of this detail had been included in the gospels, but it was not!

Some sociologists and politicians believe that many of the ills in modern society are due to the breakdown of family life. It is easy to blame not only society's problems but also our own difficulties or weaknesses on faults in our own family background and it is not only singles who do this. However, some people do remain single because they have been so damaged by hurts and experiences in their childhood that they find mature, trusting relationships virtually impossible.

Facing up to the past

Part of growing up is to recognize that parents are not infallible and to be ready to forgive the shortcomings we have had to endure. As Christians, forgiveness should be easier for us because we have already experienced God's forgiveness for our own weaknesses and sins. Forgiving others is often difficult, but in his teaching on the Lord's Prayer, Jesus makes our own forgiveness by him conditional on our forgiving others (Matthew 6:14). A high standard indeed!

God wants us to be whole people, and that may mean facing up to our past, perhaps with the help of others, whether through counselling, inner healing or in whatever way God leads us. As Paul put it, 'When I was a child, I talked like a child, I thought like a child, I reasoned like a child. When I became a man, I put childish ways behind me' (1 Corinthians 13:11). He was illustrating the difference between what we know of God now and what it will be like to 'see face to face' (verse 12), but this growth away from childhood is important for us all. Jesus had to do it too, so he can help those of us who find it a difficult process.

No family

The Old Testament makes it clear that God has a special interest in those who are humanly speaking without a family. His concern for them appears in the laws that governed the behaviour of the people of Israel: 'Do not take advantage of a widow or an orphan. If you do and they cry out to me, I will certainly hear their cry. My anger will be aroused . . .' (Exodus 22:22–24). The theme is repeated again and again, in the law, the Psalms and the Prophets. I particularly like Psalm 68:5–6, 'A father to the fatherless, a defender of widows, is God in his holy dwelling. God sets the lonely in families . . .'. How people cared for the fatherless and widows was frequently a measure of the justice in the society of the time, and a cause for judgment (e.g. Isaiah 10:2). His concern did not cease at the end of Old Testament times.

Was Jesus' concern for widows born out of seeing his mother experience widowhood? Luke told us that Anna was a widow (2:37), included the story of the widow of Nain whose son Jesus raised from the dead (7:12), and noticed the widow putting two tiny coins into the temple treasury (21:2). Jesus was certainly interested in members of society who were frequently ignored or excluded, and as we will see in chapter 12, we can experience this same concern when we are in need of it.

Misunderstanding

Jesus faced another struggle with his family when he began his ministry. He left Nazareth and made his base in Capernaum (Mark 2:1). His family did not understand at all what he was doing: they thought he had gone 'out of his mind', and went to 'take charge of him' (Mark 3:21). John made a point of telling us that 'even his own brothers did not believe in him' (John 7:5), although they obviously did later because they were there in the upper room (Acts 1:14) and one of them, James, was a leader in the Jerusalem church (Acts 15:13 etc.).

Those who choose singleness for the sake of the kingdom of heaven may find themselves misunderstood by their family, who want to see them 'settle down', in other words get married! No one is excused from the biblical command to honour our father and mother (Matthew 19:19; Ephesians 6:2), but Jesus taught that putting him first may result in being 'betrayed even by parents, brothers, relatives and friends' (Luke 21:16). On one occasion Jesus clearly told his disciples that his coming would result in families dividing against each other (Luke 12:52 –53). In a literal sense, this is a common experience for those who live under repressive governments, and it is a danger that those in Muslim lands must face up to when they consider the claims of Christ.

Putting Christ first in our lives may be costly. We saw in chapter one that it may mean renouncing marriage: it may also mean losing our family. This can happen in more than one way: Paul allows for a situation where one partner is a Christian and the other is not and chooses to leave (1 Corinthians 7:15).

The church as family

However, it is not all bad news. Even though we may lose out as far as our human family is concerned, when we become Christians, we gain a family! Jesus himself tells us that 'no-one who has left home or brothers or sisters or mother or father or children or fields for me and the gospel will fail to receive a hundred times as much in this present age (homes, brothers, sisters, mothers, children and fields . . .)' (Mark 10:29–30). Some commentators take this to mean that Jesus envisaged the re-creation of family relationships, through the formation of the church.

Paul uses the word family as one of his many and varied descriptions of the church. In Galatians 6 he gives some teaching on our responsibilities towards one another, which he concludes, 'Therefore, as we have opportunity, let us do good to all people, especially to those who belong to the family of believers' (verse 10). 'Family' here is not the nuclear family of parents and children, nor even the extended family of blood relatives; it is a household which includes all kinds of people. Paul uses the same idea again when writing to the Ephesians: 'You are no longer foreigners and aliens, but . . . members of God's household' (2:19). As members of this family or household we can expect to have relationships which include us all, whether married or single, elderly or young, parent, child or childless.

In parts of the world where a new Christian is ostracized by his or her natural family, it is important that a young believer finds a new family. It is also important in societies where the extended family principle is strong. People who have always expected their tribal leader or family head to play a major part in decision making should not be expected to cope on their own. Several co-operative projects between Missions have recognized this in recent years, and some imaginative programmes of outreach and follow-up are resulting in people turning to Christ and growing as Christians in some very tough places.

The breakdown of marriages and disintegration of family life means that many new Christians come into our churches having had a bad experience of family life. Part of their wholeness as new creations in Christ is to experience the love and care which they may not have had in their home. God planned that the best environment in which to grow to human maturity is a secure, loving family. It is spiritually too!

In Britain we nominally recognize that a church should be a family, but in practice the word is frequently used unconsciously to mean only the nuclear family. A 'Family Service' at its worst can be simply an excuse for the Sunday School teachers to have a week off, while frustrated parents try to keep children quiet in an adult service. As often as not such a service also provides an excuse for many single, childless and elderly people to have a Sunday off too. What a shame! Children need to be part of the whole church from time to time, and to feel included in worship, whatever form that may take, but not to the exclusion of others. A 'Family Service' should include the whole family of that church, whatever age, whether married or single, even though it may not be possible for all of them to be represented in the same service.

Let us live as 'members of God's household' (Ephesians 2:19) so that everyone can play their part in family life, and each of us be 'built together to become a dwelling in which God lives by his Spirit' (Ephesians 2:22).

Questions

1. In what ways was my own family life imperfect? What needs has that created in me and in what ways might Jesus meet them?

2. Since church is meant to be 'family', what can I do to improve the sense of family in my church?

7

Home and security

My grandfather went to visit two elderly ladies, who invited him in saying, 'Please make yourself at home: it's so much nicer for us when you're at home'! It has been a family joke ever since, because it plays on two of the meanings of the word 'home'. The dictionary adds these and others: 'the place where a person or family lives; the city, region, or country where one was born or reared; a restful or congenial place where one likes to be'.

In the last chapter we thought about family. However, family and home are not necessarily the same thing. Although Jesus continued to have a human family, he left home when his ministry began. In Luke chapter 4 we find him in the synagogue at Nazareth 'where he had been brought up' (verse 16), but his time there ended when the people 'drove him out of the town' (verse 28). He probably never went back to his family home again, although he continued to be known as 'Jesus of Nazareth' (e.g. Luke 24:19; Acts 4:10).

Jesus has been accused of being against homes because he said, 'the Son of Man has nowhere to lay his head' (Matthew 8:20). However, there is evidence in the gospels that Jesus had another home during his ministry. When he first left Nazareth, 'he went and lived in Capernaum' (Matthew 4:13). John the Baptist's two disciples asked him where he was staying and he took them there for the day (John 1:37–39). Mark tells us that the townspeople of Capernaum recognized that his home was among them (Mark 2:1). In his account the paralysed man who is brought to Jesus by four friends is actually lowered through the roof of Jesus' home (Mark 2:1–12)!

Jesus not only had his own home base, he also visited other people's homes: he was in Peter's home when he healed Peter's mother-in-law (Matthew 8:14), and he visited the home of Martha, Mary and Lazarus on various occasions.

A home of my own

A home is important for us all; somewhere where we belong – 'a restful and congenial place where one likes to be', as the dictionary puts it. Until recent times the extended family was the norm, as it was in Jesus' day. Even in industrialized societies in the past most young people lived 'at home' with their parents until they married, and that is still true in many parts of the world. However, increasingly young people everywhere want to leave home, and move out on their own. Perhaps there are better job opportunities or training elsewhere, or they go away to university, enjoy the freedom and do not want to return to live with their parents. Children whose parents have divorced and remarried often feel unwelcome or uncomfortable with the new relationship and may escape from the situation by moving out as soon as possible. For various reasons there are many more single people than there used to be, who have never been married but are not living with their parents. What does the concept of 'home' mean for them?

A home is more than somewhere to keep one's belongings and to sleep at night. It is to do with feeling comfortable and secure, having a place where I can express my personality and where I can be myself. Any of us can make a home almost anywhere if we want to; it may be only one room, in my case for many years in a nurses' home or a house owned by the Mission, but it is our attitude rather than our possessions that creates a home, whether it is one room or a mansion.

Contrary to many single people's expectations, getting married does not automatically provide a real home, though it can lead to a more permanent place to live. Many single people need to be encouraged to create a home and be given help and advice on the best way to do that in their circumstances. For some that means sharing a flat with a friend, others may prefer to live with a family, while some are quite happy living alone if they can afford to do so.

It is different for people who have been married and bereaved; together with a partner they have built a home, but when that partner dies, the place where they live may no longer feel like home. For the divorced, home may have been a battleground rather than a secure place for a long time and in any divorce one, if not both, partners will have had to move out of the home they used to share.

Making a new life alone after the end of a marriage often needs to include learning to feel 'at home' again in the new circumstances. One aspect of this is acquiring the skills which the other partner previously contributed to the home like shopping, keeping accounts, simple house maintenance and cooking. This is one way in which the church can show sensitive practical support.

I know of a man who had hardly ever cooked a meal for himself before his wife died. He was very grateful for meals provided by friends, but what he appreciated most was the person who came in once a week and taught him how to cook! He and his wife had always enjoyed inviting friends to their home for a meal: soon he felt confident enough in his cooking to once again open his home to friends. For him that was a big step forward in his new life alone.

Homes are important

In the Bible we find various examples of the importance of homes. When Jesus sent out the disciples in Matthew 10, he gave them specific instructions about where they should stay. They could not of course book in at the local hotel; they had no choice but to stay in people's homes. To Jesus the home they selected represented the whole community, which would either receive a blessing or judgment, according to how the visiting disciples were treated (Matthew 10:11–15).

There were no church buildings in New Testament times. In Acts we find the believers 'broke bread in their homes and ate together' (2:46), and there are numerous examples of the travelling apostles receiving hospitality. One example is Lydia at Philippi: 'When she and the members of her household were baptised, she invited us to her home' (Acts 16:15). When Paul wrote to the church at Rome he could say of Gaius, 'whose hospitality I and the whole church here enjoy' (Romans 16:23). Paul commanded the Christians at Rome to practise hospitality (12:13), and there is no indication that anyone was excused that command! When Paul sent guidelines to Timothy about the selection of church leaders, hospitality was among the list of required characteristics, sandwiched between qualities which we might rate more highly, such as self-control and the ability to teach (1 Timothy 3:2).

Single people can be very poor at hospitality, and a

frequent complaint is that they are not invited out for meals. My response is often, 'When did you last invite people to Sunday lunch, or a dinner party?' For many years a friend and I had an arrangement that if neither of us had any other invitation, we would have Sunday lunch together. Even if we do not have very much, sharing it can be a blessing. Remember the young boy who provided the loaves and fish for the feeding of the five thousand. Who knows, we may even entertain angels without knowing it (Hebrews 13:2)!

Forgoing a home

It is good to be able to feel at home and provide an environment where others can also feel relaxed, but if as Christians our security depends on geographical location, then something is wrong. When I left Radio Worldwide I went to live with my parents temporarily and so moved away not only from the team but also from my church and most of my friends. Within a few months my parents moved to another part of the country and then I went to university for a year before taking up a new job. Four moves in two years certainly tested where my security lay!

Matthew 8:20 is often quoted when we think of where Jesus lived, 'Foxes have holes and birds of the air have nests, but the Son of Man has nowhere to lay his head'. He included homes in the list of things we may be called upon to give up for the sake of the kingdom of God (Luke 18:29). Jesus used an unexpected illustration when he was forced to leave Nazareth. He quoted the famous saying about a prophet not being without honour except in his home town, and then he went on to remind his listeners that both Elijah and Elisha ministered to people who were not Israelites. Elijah spent three and a half years of severe famine living with a widow in Zarephath, nowhere near his home area, while Elisha was instrumental in the healing of Naaman, a Syrian (Luke 4:24–27).

Jesus still asks some people to give up home, or at least have one in a place different from where they might have chosen, in order to serve him. What about those who stay in, or deliberately move to, an inner city area in order to support a church and its witness there? Those who go to foreign countries often have to live in accommodation quite different from what they left behind 'at home'. Yet with some thought and care in both cases it is possible to turn the new environment into a home where local people feel welcome and comfortable and there is a sense of security and belonging.

At home in God

There is another aspect to the idea of home that has nothing to do with where we live. Jesus said that when we love and obey him 'My Father will love him, and we will come to him and make our home with him' (John 14:23). Paul talked about Christ dwelling in our hearts, the Good News version puts it, 'I pray that Christ will make his home in your hearts through faith' (Ephesians 3:17). What an amazing thought, that God can feel 'at home' in us! Jesus' prayer in John 17 makes it clear that this is a two-way relationship, 'just as you are in me and I am in you. May they also be in us . . .' (verse 21).

If we really feel at home in our relationship with God and with his Son Jesus Christ, then it does not matter where we live. People like Corrie Ten Boom have illustrated these truths by the way they were able to live in dreadful circumstances, in her case as a prisoner in a concentration camp.

Psalm 84 gives us a lovely, practical illustration: we can be as at home in God's presence as a sparrow or swallow is in its nest! The Psalmist must have seen the nests of sparrows and swallows in the temple and it made him want for himself the same sense of God's nearness. He longed with the whole of his being to be in God's presence, 'How lovely is your dwelling-place, O LORD Almighty! My soul yearns, even faints, for the courts of the LORD; my heart and my flesh cry out for the living God.' It was not a vain hope, he knew that 'Blessed are those who dwell in your house; they are ever praising you' (Psalm 84:1–4). We too can build our nest in God's presence, like the sparrow and swallow.

Isaiah gave a wonderful description of what life will be like when 'the Spirit is poured upon us from on high' (Isaiah 32:15). One of the blessings is 'secure homes . . . undisturbed places of rest' (verse 18). There is also Jesus' promise that he would prepare a place for us in his Father's house (John 14:2), even if we never have a home of our own here on earth, we will have a wonderful one in heaven. Won't that be thrilling!

Finding our security primarily in our relationship with God is an important part of Christian maturity. The security of young children revolves around their home and parents. As we grow up all sorts of other things can become the basis of our security: job, possessions, money, a particular relationship, even our home. Knowing God in an intimate and personal way gives a much firmer foundation. Being aware that he is 'at home' in my heart and that 'in him we live and move and have our being' (Acts 17:28) can help us remain secure even if outward circumstances are unsettling.

Questions

1. Where do I feel at home? How can I help others to feel at home?

2. Would I be willing to give up my home if God asked me to, perhaps to move to an inner city or to another country?

3. What is the basis of my security? Do I ever feel insecure, and if so, how can I let God meet my need for security?

8

Alone versus lonely

The phrase 'home alone' looks set to become part of the English language since the films of that name and the incidents subsequent to them. There was a public outcry that parents could think of leaving young children alone and without supervision for days at a time. Yet at some point in their lives many people have to learn to live alone: in 1990 just over one in four of all households in the United Kingdom was occupied by one person, compared to one in ten in 1951. That meant about a sixth of all adults were living by themselves, an awful lot of people to be home alone.

In 1992 the *Singularly Significant* survey showed that on average one in three church members was a single adult, with a higher proportion in some areas, especially inner cities. These single people cited loneliness as a problem more often than any other issue. For many, loneliness is at times almost overwhelming and they identify with the meaninglessness of it that Solomon described: 'There was a man all alone; he had neither son nor brother. There was no end to his toil, yet his eyes were not content with his wealth . . . this too is meaningless—a miserable business!' (Ecclesiastes 4:8).

Loneliness is especially devastating after a divorce, bereavement or broken engagement. It is poignant for the bereaved if those they thought were friends stay away when they are needed most, perhaps because they do not know what to say. Yet it is not only singles who face loneliness: many married people, especially mothers of young children, are very lonely and long for the time and freedom to go out and meet people.

Lost in the crowd

Single people tend to be refreshed by other people in order to cope when they are alone. For Jesus it was the other way round. The gospels give the impression that he was constantly on the move, always at the heart of the action. Mark underlines this by frequently using the words 'immediately' or 'straightaway'. Everywhere he went crowds of people followed him. Yet at times he needed to withdraw from the crowd; to be alone to pray and be renewed before he returned to them.

Yet being alone and being lonely are not necessarily synonymous: it is equally possible to be quite content with your own company, or devastatingly lonely and lost in a crowd. In a large crowd or a bustling street it is easy to feel that nobody knows I am here, and nobody would notice if I were not, nobody knows how I feel or is interested in what I do. This is particularly true in the busy anonymity of a big city where work colleagues may live miles away and neighbours keep themselves to themselves.

All individuals

Jesus did not see crowds as an anonymous mass of people; rather, 'When he saw the crowds, he had compassion on them, because they were harassed and helpless, like sheep without a shepherd' (Matthew 9:36). Various parables show how important one individual is to God. Probably the best known are the ones in Luke 15: the lost coin, the lost sheep and the prodigal son. As he travelled the country, Jesus repeatedly picked out individuals in particular need, such as the lame man at the pool of Bethesda (John 5:3, 5), or blind Bartimaeus (Mark 10:46–52). He preached to massive crowds, and yet he called each of his disciples individually.

There are billions of people in the world, and millions of Christians, yet Jesus deals with us all individually. When he said to his disciples, 'whoever acknowledges me before men, the Son of Man will also acknowledge him before the angels of God' (Luke 12:8), he was speaking in the singular, not the plural. When the seventy-two returned from their preaching and healing tour, they were thrilled at what they had seen. However, Jesus' response was, 'do not rejoice that the spirits submit to you, but rejoice that your names are written in heaven' (Luke 10:20). All they had witnessed was not as important as the fact that their own names, individually, were written in heaven.

Before God we are not just one of the crowd, each of us is an individual whom he knows so intimately that he knows how many hairs we have on our head (Matthew 10:30). We come to faith in him one by one; he speaks to us personally through the Bible and in other ways; he answers our prayers and gives his Spirit 'to each one' (1 Corinthians 12:7). Jesus is the Good Shepherd, who 'calls his own sheep by name and leads them out'. He says 'I know my sheep' (John 10:3, 14). When God speaks to us, he does so in our own language, and he knows where to find us! We cannot be lost in the crowd as far as Jesus is concerned.

This of course is true for everyone, not only singles. It is equally relevant to the 'church widow', whose partner does not share her faith, and indeed to all married couples: people whose Christian life depends on their spouse are in danger of losing their faith as well as their companion if they are widowed or divorced.

In a lonely or isolated situation it is very easy to become convinced that nobody cares. Elijah did! After the demonstration of God's power on Mount Carmel and his subsequent killing of the prophets of Baal, Elijah found himself on the run from Queen Jezebel. At last, after a stop in the desert when he was so exhausted that he wanted to die, he reached Mount Horeb. There God spoke to him, not in the earthquake, fire or wind, but in a gentle whisper. Twice God asked him, 'What are you doing here Elijah?' (1 Kings 19:9, 13). On both occasions, Elijah gave exactly the same answer: it must have been engraved on his mind from constant repetition over the preceding weeks! He was the total pessimist: everything had gone wrong and his complaint ended with the pitiful 'I am the only one left, and now they are trying to kill me too.' Sometimes loneliness can create similar feelings for us.

What Elijah had completely forgotten was that only a short time before he had met Obadiah, a devout believer in the Lord (18:3). Obadiah had told Elijah that he had hidden one hundred prophets of the Lord to protect them from Jezebel's murderous plans. No, if Elijah had stopped to think about it, he would have known that he was not the only one left. But that was how he felt.

God did not condemn him; he sent him back with some specific tasks to carry out, and with the commission to anoint Elisha to succeed him. A delightful extra is that God told Elijah how totally wrong he was to think he was the only one left; the real number of those who had remained faithful to him was not 102 (himself, Obadiah and the 100 in the cave) but 7,000! Elijah had no justification whatsoever for his tale of woe – and neither do we if we can think about it dispassionately.

When we are tempted to feel nobody is interested in us, nobody understands, a thoughtful meditation on Psalm 139 is a good antidote. There King David shared his discovery that even if he wanted to, he could not run away from God. God knew where David was and where he was going, he had planned every day of his life long before he was even thought of; David could not even hide his thoughts from God! That can be rather unsettling if there are things we want to hide from God, but God actually knows us far better than anyone ever can, whether that be parent, friend, husband or wife. To experience God's presence when we are alone is not a mystical experience reserved for the hermit, it is something any one of us can know.

Being alone

There were times when Jesus wanted to be alone. One occasion was when John the Baptist had been killed by Herod. 'When Jesus heard what had happened, he withdrew by boat privately to a solitary place' (Matthew 14:13). The bereaved can take comfort from the fact that Jesus felt the need to be on his own to think about the death of his cousin. However, as so often happened, the crowds followed. Jesus could so easily have felt frustrated: he wanted to be alone. But he did not ignore them or send them away. He was never self-centred; if there were people in need he met that need, and on that occasion, the feeding of the five thousand followed.

Jesus was always thinking of others and acting to

meet their needs. It is a great temptation when we are alone, whether by deliberate choice or through force of circumstances, to become introspective; my mother used to say I was being 'President of the Poor Me Society'!

Aloneness can be positive

When Jesus needed to get away from the crowds, he sometimes took his disciples with him, recognizing that they also needed a break from the continuous pressure of people. 'Because so many people were coming and going that they did not even have a chance to eat, he said to them, "Come with me by yourselves to a quiet place and get some rest"' (Mark 6:31). However much we may want to be with other people, we cannot give out to others all the time. That is a danger for singles in leadership and pastoral positions: other people are constantly making demands on them, but there is no one at home to tell them they must stop, or must have a day off. People have sometimes asked me if I found it hard being a woman leader. For me being a single leader was much harder, for this very reason, as well as the loneliness of some of the burdens a leader cannot share.

There are times when we must be alone, not only for our own sanity, but primarily to be with God. Luke tells us that 'Jesus often withdrew to lonely places and prayed' (5:16). These were the times when he drew close to his Father. He may even have had a favourite place: 'one day Jesus was praying in a certain place' (Luke 11:1). Some people spend many, many hours on their own, especially elderly singles. Even if we would prefer not to be alone, that time can be used profitably. As with singleness itself, we may not have a choice about being alone, but we can choose our attitude to it.

Most revivals have taken place where people prayed long and earnestly. Much missionary work would have collapsed and churches fallen apart if it were not for older people who may have few physical resources left, but who spend long periods in prayer. Prayer is not easy, and there are certainly other profitable ways of using time spent alone, but if more of those hours were spent in prayer, it could change the world – and in the process change the pray-er too!

Alone, yet not alone

Jesus knew what it was to be alone at a time when he most needed support, at his trial. He knew the disciples would desert him, yet he was able to say, 'You will leave me all alone. Yet I am not alone, for my Father is with me' (John 16:32). Along with all the other things he experienced in those dreadful days, he was aware before it all started to happen that he would have no human support beside him. He understands when we feel there are things we do not know how to face on our own, because he has been through that too.

He tried to prepare his disciples for the time, not when they would leave him, but when he would leave them, to return to heaven. There would be an enormous gap in their lives: they had spent three years with him, and their lives now revolved around him. When he went away, they would be bereft: perhaps they would feel like orphans. But they would not stay that way; 'I will not leave you as orphans; I will come to you . . . my Father will love him and we will come to him' (John 14:18, 23). Knowing God's love in this way makes a tremendous difference to the loneliness of singleness.

Each of us, whether married or single, needs a personal, private relationship with God. Using at least some of our time alone to cultivate that relationship turns our thoughts and feelings away from ourselves and up to God. Then refreshed and renewed, we can look out to the needs of others, rather than concentrating exclusively on our own needs. We may continue to have a lot of time alone, but the loneliness will recede as we give some of that time to God.

Questions

1. What makes me feel lonely? How can I make better use of the time I spend alone, and encourage others to do the same?

2. When did I last spend time on my own with God and draw close to him so that he could speak to me personally?

3. Write down three things you will do in the next six months to help meet the needs of someone who is lonely. How will you go about doing these things?

9

Friends

Good friendships are another antidote to loneliness: they are something most of us want and appreciate when we have them. Several proverbs about friends come from the Bible, including these from the book of Proverbs:

> A friend loves at all times, and a brother is born for adversity (17:17).

> A man that hath friends must show himself friendly (18:24 KJV).

> Faithful are the wounds of a friend (27:6 KJV).

We find various friendships in the Bible; perhaps the best known is the one between David and Jonathan. On several occasions that friendship saved David from being murdered by Jonathan's father, King Saul. They even made a covenant with one another to confirm their friendship (1 Samuel 20:16–17). Many years after Jonathan's death in battle, David asked, 'Is there anyone still left of the house of Saul to whom I can show kindness for Jonathan's sake?' (2 Samuel 9:1). He discovered that there was a disabled son, Mephibosheth, who himself had a son. David's loyalty to Jonathan meant that Mephibosheth was given back his father's land, and from then on he lived in Jerusalem and ate at the king's table.

David and Jonathan's friendship was a very deep one, but it is not the only one we find in the Bible. Doctor Luke travelled extensively with Paul and was his close companion through many adventures and hardships. Paul calls him 'our dear friend' (Colossians 4:14). Timothy was also on the same journeys, but Paul had a different relationship with him; he was 'my true son in the faith' (1 Timothy 1:2). In Romans 16, Paul named over thirty people whom he either sent greetings to or passed on greetings from, and some of them he called friends.

John wrote his third epistle to a close friend, Gaius, whom he loved so much that he called him 'dear friend' four times in fourteen verses!

The Twelve

Perhaps the best example of a wide range of friends is yet again the Lord Jesus Christ. He had one particularly close companion, a group of three, twelve disciples, a number of women who had followed him from Galilee and others whose homes he visited.

In those days the relationship between a religious teacher and his disciples was usually remote and austere. Not so with Jesus. He was not a cold, aloof personality: it is obvious from the gospel narrative that the Twelve not only followed Jesus out of a sense of duty because he had called them, but because they wanted to. They actually enjoyed it; he was a nice person to be with, as well as a good teacher. True, he could also be uncomfortable at times – it was embarrassing when he overturned the tables of the money-changers – but he allowed them to rub the ears of corn for a quick snack when they were out walking in the countryside, even though it was the Sabbath!

Within the Twelve, three were closer friends, Peter, James and John. He took them with him on several occasions, such as when he went to heal Jairus's daughter (Luke 8:51), when he was transfigured (Luke 9:28) and in the Garden of Gethsemane (Matthew 26:37). Mark implies that Jesus' teaching on the end of the age was given only to these three, though Matthew records that all the disciples were there. They certainly had a closer relationship with Jesus than the other nine. Perhaps Jesus enjoyed the stimulation of their company: Peter, outspoken and straightforward and James and John, the 'sons of thunder'.

He had one even closer friendship, with John, 'the disciple whom Jesus loved' (John 13:23; 19:26; 20:2; 21:7, 20). The last reference suggests that all the disciples thought of John as the one whom Jesus loved. The only time John took advantage of that relationship was at the Last Supper when Peter asked him to find out who was going to betray Jesus. Jesus' answer could have been spoken quietly into John's ear, which would explain why none of the disciples understood what was going on between Jesus and Judas. Jesus clearly trusted John because during the crucifixion he handed over responsibility for his mother to John, surely not a spur of the moment decision.

Other friends

Outside the Twelve, Jesus had a range of friends, of both sexes and from right across the social spectrum of his time. Among his followers were women who had followed him from Galilee to care for his needs, including Mary Magdalene and Mary the mother of James and John (Matthew 27:55–56). Knowing Jesus as we do, it is impossible to imagine that he ignored them or treated them as servants; they did what they did because they wanted to. These women were a wonderful mixture, just as we find in many churches today! Mary, the mother of James and John, may have had an ulterior motive of keeping an eye on her sons (Matthew 20:20–21)! Mary Magdalene had been demon-possessed and therefore virtually an outcast from society and was almost certainly single. It was Mary Magdalene who was the first to see Jesus after the resurrection (John 20:10–18); what a tremendous privilege for a single woman with a very chequered history!

Also travelling with him were Joanna and Susanna (Luke 8:2–3). Joanna was married and her husband was the manager of Herod's household so she was from almost the other end of the social scale and would never have worked with Mary Magdalene under normal circumstances. In contrast, nothing is said about Susanna, yet she was among those who used their own means to help support Jesus and his disciples. This has led some people to believe that she was a wealthy widow. Two very different single women and two very different married women buried their differences because of their commitment to Jesus!

He also had friends other than those who travelled with him, most notably Mary, Martha and Lazarus. Lazarus is assumed to have been single because there is no mention of a wife, even when he died. Yet he was almost certainly old enough to be married, perhaps a contemporary of Jesus, in his early thirties. Lazarus lived in Judea, an area Jesus had previously left as too dangerous but was prepared to go back to when his friend died (John 11:7–8). At the tomb he was so moved by the emotion of the occasion that the mourners commented on how much Jesus must have loved Lazarus (verse 36).

Much has been written about Martha's busyness

when Mary sat at Jesus' feet listening to what he said (Luke 10:38–42). One commentator suggests that Martha may have been a widow, but whatever her circumstances, one is left in no doubt that she was in charge (John 12:2). It was no small thing to have thirteen men turn up on the doorstep, no doubt eager for a good meal – and they could not phone up in advance to let her know they were coming! She must have coped all right in spite of her complaint about Mary, because Jesus felt able to make their home his base during the last week of his life (Matthew 21:17). How many friends do you have who could take such an invasion in their stride?!

Mary was the third member of the household. At the dinner given in honour of Jesus after Lazarus was raised from the dead, Mary anointed Jesus with a pint of expensive perfume. It was worth about a year's wages, but more than that, many commentators agree that it was her dowry. She would have been saving it for her wedding day but she extravagantly lavished it on Jesus in a gesture of pure love.

A variety of friendships

Among Jesus' friends were men and women, single people and married (Peter must have been married because he had a mother-in-law), young and older, rich and poor. As a complete man, he needed women around him as well as men. He was comfortable with the opposite sex. That was something it took me a while to learn, having gone to all-girls schools, become a nurse, a predominantly female occupation, and been to a ladies-only Bible College. Jesus allowed Mary to sit at his feet and learn from him and he also enjoyed conversation with women. The woman at the well in John 4 was a very different character from

Mary and one we could hardly call his friend; yet he was happy to talk to her, something the disciples found surprising, presumably because they recognized what sort of woman she was (verse 27). He had been equally comfortable talking to Nicodemus who, as a Pharisee and member of the Jewish ruling council, was from the opposite end of the social scale (John 3:1).

What about friendships for single people these days? Many find them difficult and shy away from them. Others try to find in friendship all the support and companionship that they hoped to have had in marriage, or have missed since the loss of a partner. No friendship should be asked to carry that much weight, as I have discovered to my cost, having been on both ends of that kind of relationship. We need a wide range of friends who can broaden our perspectives and widen our horizons, who can bring into our lives aspects of human experience and understanding which we will never gain for ourselves. It doesn't necessarily just happen; as Proverbs reminded us, in order to have friends we must show ourselves friendly.

There are obvious pitfalls to be avoided in friendships: they can become exclusive and many unfortunate affairs started out as valued and wholesome friendships. Friendships are also subject to more change than marriages, as one of the parties moves away to get a new job, or gets married. Nevertheless friendships are important and some single people may need help to know how to build them and how to spot the potential dangers.

'My friends'

Before we leave the subject of friends, we cannot

overlook Jesus' teaching in John 15. There he says quite a remarkable thing to his disciples, 'You are my friends if you do what I command. I no longer call you servants, because a servant does not know his master's business. Instead, I have called you friends, for everything that I learned from my Father I have made known to you' (verses 14–15). That is amazing! We need to follow Jesus' example and have a wide range of human friendships, but we can go further than that and know Jesus as a friend.

What is true friendship? Surely it is a sharing of ourselves and of experiences which mutually enrich each other. Jesus did not want disciples who behaved like servants, simply doing as they were told without any understanding of why. He does not want followers like that now either. Then, he told his disciples what he knew and much of the gospels consists of this teaching. Now, he still wants people who will not only learn from him in an academic sense, but who will open up to him emotionally and become his friends.

There are people in Scripture who were described as friends of God. Abraham is probably the best known: God called him 'my friend' (Isaiah 41:8), and James quoted that as part of his argument that a person is justified by what he does and not by faith alone (James 2:23). Moses was another: 'The Lord would speak to Moses face to face, as a man speaks with his friend' (Exodus 33:11). Jeremiah called the Lord 'my Father, my friend from my youth' (3:4). The word friend is not actually used to describe David's relationship with God, but he is called a man after God's own heart (1 Samuel 13:14), and someone 'who enjoyed God's favour' (Acts 7:46). We too can have a friendship with God which, along with human friendships, can meet many of our needs for companionship.

Questions

1. Take a sheet of paper and write your own name in the middle. Write the names of your friends around your name, the distance from your own illustrating how close they are to you. Are these friends a good cross-section of the people with whom you are acquainted? Do they include a wide range of people, old and young, male and female, similar background and different? Which friendships need to be worked on?

2. Spend some time thanking God for your friends and praying for each of them.

3. Do I know someone who appears to have no friends? How can I help them?

10

Sex and sexuality

I used to teach a Bible Class of teenage girls. One Sunday one of them from a Christian home came to me and said, 'All my friends are sleeping with their boyfriends. I know I shouldn't, but why shouldn't I?' Was she justified in thinking most of her friends were involved in sexual activity? A survey by Carrick James Market Research in 1990 shows that she probably was. The study covered 761 16–24-year-olds, 85 per cent of whom claimed to have had at least one sexual partner in the previous twelve months, with 11 per cent of these having had more than one.

Sexual standards for Christians

Most Christians subscribe at least in theory to the teaching by Jesus and Paul that sexual practice is only permitted within marriage. Jesus was quite clear that he had 'not come to abolish the Law or the Prophets . . . but to fulfil them' (Matthew 5:17). He was unequivocal about the command, 'Do not commit adultery': to him, breaking that law began not with the sexual act, but the lustful look (5:28). If there was any room for doubt about what Jesus meant, he dispelled it when he said 'out of the heart come . . . adultery, sexual immorality . . . these are what make a man "unclean"' (Matthew 15:19). Paul drove home the same message on numerous occasions (e.g. 1 Corinthians 6:18; 2 Corinthians 12:21; Galatians 5:19; Ephesians 5:3 etc.). It is also interesting to reflect on the fact that if there is no need for marriage in heaven, there will be no sexual activity there either!

My teenage friend knew these biblical standards, but what she really wanted to know was not 'why?', but 'how' not to! That is a question many single people struggle with, myself included. James makes it clear that there is a process involved in yielding to temptation: 'each one is tempted when, by his own evil desire, he is dragged away and enticed. Then, after desire has conceived, it gives birth to sin; and sin, when it is full-grown, gives birth to death' (James 1:14–15). This downward spiral applies just as much to sexual temptation as to any other; perhaps more so because the sexual drive can be so strong. It is possible to escape from it however, the sooner the better!

It has been said that the most important sex organ in the body is the brain, so it is hardly surprising to find Paul writing that the starting point for dealing with sexual temptation is our thoughts: 'put aside the deeds of darkness . . . orgies . . . sexual immorality and debauchery . . . rather, clothe yourselves with the Lord Jesus Christ, and do not think about how to gratify the desires of the sinful nature' (Romans 13:12–14). When our lives are fully committed to Christ and our spirit is under the control of the Holy Spirit, then our spirit should govern what we think rather than the other way round.

We need to think through these issues and make decisions in the cold light of day about our behaviour. Setting personal limits in advance considerably reduces the possibility of being 'dragged away and enticed' by our desires. It is no good hoping that we will do the right thing when temptation comes along. The limits set need to include keeping clear of unnecessary temptation, which means recognizing where our own weaknesses lie. I do not read romantic novels nor watch films that are passionate love stories because for me they can arouse desires that are difficult to control. Joseph set a good example: when Potiphar's wife tried to lure him into bed with her, he fled. He knew that yielding to the temptation would be a sin not only against his master, but also against God (Genesis 39:9). In the popular musical *Joseph and the Amazing Technicolour Dreamcoat* this story is changed to bring it into line with current behaviour, a fate that befalls a lot of Christian teaching on sex!

For some time there has been a growing awareness that the church needs to teach Christian standards of morality and sexual behaviour to its young people. However there is a strange attitude towards older single people, as though they are somehow sexless beings; sex outside marriage is forbidden, so therefore it is not a problem! But for many it is a hard struggle, particularly for those who want to live up to God's standards but who have already experienced a sexual relationship. What does the church have to say that can help, other than 'Don't do it'?

Teaching on subjects such as holiness, forgiveness and purity in all dimensions of life and letting God renew our minds is all relevant to enabling both singles and marrieds to live sexually pure lives. However, there is another dimension to the discussion which is often overlooked.

Sexuality is more than sex

Before the fall, Adam and Eve were sexual beings, 'So God created man in his own image, in the image of God he created him; male and female he created them' (Genesis 1:27). Their sexuality was included when 'God saw all that he had made, and it was very

85

good' (verse 31). It could be argued that sex only became such a powerful drive after the fall, when part of Eve's penalty was, 'Your desire will be for your husband, and he will rule over you' (Genesis 3:16). But we need to put the subject in its context: sexual intercourse is a strong expression of sexuality, but it is far from being the only one.

The world lives as though the sexual act and sexuality are virtually the same thing, though even secular psychologists tell us that they are not. The sexual act is out of limits for committed Christians except with a marriage partner, but fortunately other aspects of our sexuality are not.

The desire for sex is a powerful drive; however, Jesus lived a pure and holy life, untainted by any even slightly immoral relationship, whatever some modern writers and movie-makers declare. The writer to the Hebrews tells us that Jesus was 'tempted in every way, just as we are—yet was without sin', so he is able to 'sympathise with our weaknesses' (4:15). He understands the temptation for a man to look with lust at a pretty woman; he recognized it as a common experience. I am sure he also understands the similar longing for a sexual partner which can almost overwhelm a single woman, particularly at certain times of the month. Jesus was fully human; the fact that he set high standards of sexual behaviour does not mean he was a sexless being: he expressed his sexuality in other ways. If he can live without 'it', he can enable singles now to do so too.

Ignoring or repressing sexual desires is not the answer. We need rather to find positive ways to cope with them or replace them. A significant step forward for me was to realize that there are ways to express other aspects of masculinity or femininity. Many of us have grown up with pictorial images of 'gentle Jesus, meek and mild' and imagine him as a weak, even effeminate man. Far from it! It is inconceivable that someone who had been a carpenter for perhaps fifteen years was not physically strong. We only have to look at him in the temple courts turning out the money-changers and the men who were selling cattle, sheep and doves. Visualize the havoc he wrought as he exercised all his male strength and aggression in that situation. He could be 'macho' when he needed to be, yet he also displayed the compassion and sensitivity of the so-called 'New Man'. Nowhere does Jesus' life even suggest that men should not be fully masculine in their attitudes and behaviour.

Many people have pointed out how he gave women a status way beyond that of their time. Luke's gospel, in particular shows how Jesus respected women and in many ways he treated them as equals, healing them, sharing hospitality and speaking to them in the same way as he did to men. Christian women can live out to the full their femaleness – though what that means has been interpreted in a wide range of ways! Nevertheless, even a short visit to other parts of the world brings home vividly the different way women are treated in countries which have a Christian heritage from those which have not. A report published in the USA in 1988 puts another side of the picture: 'More than 60% of women and girls in the world live under conditions that threaten their health, deny them choice about childbearing, limit educational attainment, restrict economic participation and fail to guarantee them equal rights and freedom with men.' Being a Christian allows women to be feminine, even if some are uneasy about being feminist.

Creativity

Another way to cope with sexual desire is to find ways of replacing it. An important aspect of the sexual drive is the need we all have within us to be creative. We are made in the image of God and as soon as we open the first page of the Bible we find God expressing that creativity as he made the universe with all its lavish variety. He was, and is, supremely creative without that having any sexual overtones.

Jesus demonstrated creative sides to his personality. I would love to step back in time and watch him at work in his carpenter's shop. I am sure he knew how to choose the best wood, and how to carve it to make the most of its strength. When he said to his followers, 'my yoke is easy' (Matthew 11:28), he used a deliberate play on words: anyone who had bought one of his yokes for their oxen knew they fitted well, with no chafing or rubbing.

He was creative too in his approach to people: consider some of the methods he used. When he healed the deaf mute, he used spit (Mark 7:33), as he did with the blind man at Bethsaida (Mark 8:23) and the man blind from birth (John 9:6)! In Jesus' day the saliva of a firstborn was thought to heal diseases of the eye, but only on one of those three occasions did Jesus use it in the prescribed way. The other twice he did something different.

His use of language was brilliantly creative, something I particularly appreciate because my own expression of creativity is often through the spoken word, by radio. His discussions and debates with the Jewish leaders often left them hopelessly caught out by his clever reasoning. He made the most of his knowledge of who he was, of Old Testament

Scriptures, and of the teaching of the Pharisees and Sadducees, at times playing one off against the other to emerge unscathed from their cleverly devised traps. John's gospel gives us chapter after chapter of wonderful examples.

Singles should be encouraged to develop the creative side of their personality and consciously to see that as a significant aspect of sexuality. What each of us can create varies enormously, whether it be a beautiful painting, a colourful garden, an expressive poem or a delicious meal. As we work on such tasks, we need to remind ourselves that doing them is an expression of the need we all have to be creative.

Variety

Another aspect of creativity is variety. I often look at nature and wonder at the lavishness of God's creation. He did not *have* to create so many different kinds of birds, or give such a range of colour to flowers – colours which never clash as man-made colours can! Jesus observed nature (he had made it!) and employed his observations in many of his parables. He talked about sparrows and lilies of the field, grapes and wine, good and bad fruit, thorns and thistles, rock and sand and storm, sheep and shepherds and wolves . . . ! Observing the amazing natural world helps us to see the wealth of beauty it holds – a beauty which is far wider than the attractiveness of the opposite sex.

There are all sorts of ways to bring more variety into our lives and to express the personality God has given us. For example, some single people need to be challenged to be more creative in the way they dress. When I started to feel comfortable with my femininity I decided that as I was unlikely ever to wear an engagement or wedding ring, I would wear a dress ring I had inherited from my grandmother. I once knew a middle-aged single lady who could only be described by the old-fashioned word 'frumpy'. The message her clothes gave was, 'please ignore me, I'm not worth noticing'. I am sure that is not the way God wanted her to look. There are styles and colours to suit each of us, not to flaunt ourselves so as to attract the opposite sex, but to be 'me'.

Parenting

The desire to be creative is one aspect of our personalities which can find outlets other than the sexual act. Another is parenting, passing on that which we have learned of life. The creation of a child takes only a few moments, it takes nine months to bring it to birth, and twenty years or so to nurture it to maturity.

As far as we know, Paul had no natural children, but he certainly saw himself as having parental responsibilities. He wrote to the Galatians, 'my dear children, for whom I am again in the pains of childbirth until Christ is formed in you' (4:19), and he called the Corinthians 'my children' (1 Corinthians 4:14; 2 Corinthians 6:13). He described himself to the Thessalonians as both a mother and a father: 'we were gentle among you, like a mother caring for her little children' (1 Thessalonians 2:7), 'we dealt with each of you as a father deals with his own children, encouraging, comforting and urging you to live lives worthy of God' (1 Thessalonians 2:11–12).

He felt a special responsibility for Timothy, his protégé, calling him 'my true son in the faith' (1 Timothy 1:2), 'my son' (1:18; 2 Timothy 2:1), and 'my dear son' (2 Timothy 1:2). Titus and Onesimus were also accorded this special relationship (Titus 1:4; Philemon 10).

Each of us can work and pray to see Christ formed in others, and then take responsibility to see them nurtured to maturity in their faith. One of my great joys was when another member of that girls' Bible Class, who had become a Christian as a result of attending it as a teenager, later took over leadership of it. Like Paul we can be a spiritual parent to someone of any age. That may involve many traumas and heartaches, as it did for Paul, especially with the Corinthians, and as it does for most parents with their natural offspring. Parenting is not a sentimental joy – it is hard work – but singles are not excluded from it merely because they do not have their own natural children.

Perhaps the area of sexuality and relationships which singles struggle with most is the desire to love and be loved, to have an intimacy with someone who cares deeply for them. We will look at Jesus' example and teaching on this subject in chapter 14.

Christians need to show that we are not killjoys who repress our natural desires in an unhealthy way. We can deliberately develop other aspects of sexuality which release God-given creativity. Like Jesus, we can be fulfilled, whole people without experiencing the sexual act outside of marriage. This is not necessarily easy, but, as we have seen in previous chapters, neither are other demands of the Christian life!

Questions

1. List as many aspects of sexuality as you can think of. Which of these could you use, or encourage a single friend to use, to express your masculinity or femininity more fully?

2. What limits have you set yourself or do you teach
to others when it comes to sexual behaviour? Ask
God to help you be true to them.

11

Children

Certain news pictures stick in the memory, sometimes taking on a symbolism that reminds people of a whole event. It is said that almost everyone who is old enough can remember where they were when President Kennedy was assassinated. A more recent illustration comes from the Gulf War: the chilling attempt by Saddam Hussein to make himself appear as a 'nice guy' by talking to the children of some of the families he was holding hostage. Many of us remember the young lad who stood stiff and frightened as the general reached out a hand towards him.

What a different image from the picture we get in the gospels of Jesus with children! Far from trying to boost his own image by contact with children, he set out to change the way people thought about them. In his day children had an even lower status than women. Until they were twelve they were considered of no value, except perhaps for the help they could give in caring for younger siblings or looking after the family's sheep.

The value of children

Jesus changed that. To him they were more than just someone's offspring; they had a value and worth of their own. He demonstrated this to the disciples when they were arguing about which of them would be the greatest. It sounds on a par with those childish disputes, 'My Daddy's bigger than your Daddy', 'Oh no he isn't', 'Oh yes he is' (mine was taller than most!). Jesus knew what was going on between the disciples, as he always did, and 'took a little child and made him stand beside him' (Luke 9:47). By placing the child beside him, rather than in front of him, Jesus was honouring the child, saying in effect to the disciples that the status society afforded the boy was irrelevant or even completely the opposite to Jesus' perspective. As far as Jesus was concerned 'he who is least among you all—he is the greatest' (verse 48).

In Mark's account of this incident, Jesus took the child in his arms. The meaning of the Greek word is literally to cuddle. Children know when a person's interest in them is genuine and do not easily accept being cuddled by someone they feel uncomfortable with. Jesus was not simply using a child for his own purposes in teaching the disciples, the child felt welcomed by Jesus. Jesus was demonstrating the meaning of his words, 'whoever welcomes one of these little children in my name welcomes me' (Mark 9:36–37).

The disciples would not think of welcoming a child. Indeed on another occasion, they rebuked people who were bringing babies to Jesus for him to touch (Luke 18:15). That time also, Jesus affirmed the value and importance of children by saying that the kingdom of God belongs to them. He went on to point out that 'anyone who will not receive the kingdom of God like a little child will never enter it' (Luke 18:17). Children cannot do anything to earn entry into the kingdom of heaven; they cannot buy their way in, nor do great deeds which merit such a reward. Neither can adults: we must have the humility and simplicity of a child in our approach to the kingdom of heaven.

Some single people need to make a similar shift in

attitude. I know singles who will have nothing to do with children, either because they consider them irrelevant, or because they want their own so badly that they cannot see other people with youngsters without feeling jealous. Yet someone who has never been close to a child does not appreciate the simple yet profound faith that a child can have – in other people who may not deserve it, as well as in God. It can be both refreshing and challenging to see the straightforward way in which children approach God.

Learning from children

Children have a lot to teach adults. They have no inhibitions about getting as involved in praising God as they do in supporting their favourite football team! At the time of the triumphal entry into Jerusalem, the crowds shouted 'Hosanna to the Son of David' as Jesus entered the city. The children had the audacity to go on shouting, even in the temple area (Matthew 21:15). That infuriated the chief priests and teachers of the law. It is as though it were the last straw: it was bad enough that Jesus had driven out the money-changers and those selling doves, and then healed people. When they heard the children they could keep quiet no longer, and asked Jesus, 'Do you hear what these children are saying?' (verse 16). Jesus was not the least bit perturbed, indeed he even reminded them of Psalm 8:2, 'From the lips of children and infants you have ordained praise'. Some people would enjoy praising God far more if they were as uninhibited about it as children can be!

Children are not only capable of praise, they can also receive revelation, and that pleases the Father. In Matthew 11 Jesus denounced the cities in which most of his miracles had been performed, because they were so unresponsive. His condemnation of the inhabitants of those cities is chilling. However although the significance of the miracles he was doing was hidden from the wise and learned, it was revealed to little children, and Jesus added, 'Yes, Father, for this was your good pleasure' (Matthew 11:25–26).

Earlier in the chapter appears Jesus' acknowledgment that children are not always little angels! Some people could not be satisfied: they did not like the austerity of John the Baptist, but when Jesus came along and showed himself to be 'a friend of tax collectors and "sinners"', they did not like that either. He knew about the world of children because he used a children's rhyme to illustrate the contradiction, 'We played the flute for you, and you did not dance; we sang a dirge, and you did not mourn' (verse 17). That is just like children in some moods: whatever you suggest, they do not want to do it! How many singles know any children well enough to be acquainted with the games and rhymes that are 'in' in the playground?

The single people in a church are sometimes seen as free baby-sitters or suitable only to teach Sunday School. They have far more to offer than that, and it is understandable when singles rebel against being limited to these roles. But those without their own offspring do need to find opportunities to get to know children, to understand what makes them tick and to give them some of the love for which they need an outlet.

I am very grateful to the Radio Worldwide families who let me share their children. One particularly memorable occasion was when four families needed to exchange flats on the same day. My contribution was to take one teenager and five younger children for a special day out. On the train returning home another passenger asked a five-year-old whether I was their mother. She was quite bemused to be told, 'No, she's our boss'!

Just occasionally such love for children leads to a much greater commitment. One single male missionary in Nigeria brought up over sixty children over a number of years, each of whom was destitute until he took them in. Others have helped to care for the street children of Latin America whose plight has come to international attention in recent years.

Childhood memories

One of the reasons some people find it difficult to get close to children is that their own childhood was unhappy, and they do not like to be reminded of it. There is a recognition in the Bible that parents do not always live up to what they ought to be, but that God can fill the gap left in our lives. David said, 'though my father and mother forsake me, the LORD will receive me' (Psalm 27:10). In his book, *David*, John Hercus helps us see that David was speaking from bitter experience.

> His boyhood home setting was bleak and bitter and hateful . . . for he was born when his father was old – really old – as the last of a whole string of children. Not that that matters. Not in itself. But this was his father's second marriage. And mother's second marriage too. And she had a grown-up family by another husband. And along this axis it was that the whole household split clean down the middle. Split in a bloodbath of hatred and murder and general human bitterness that cost five of them their lives.
>
> (*David*, John Hercus (IVP, 1967) p.12)

97

Yes, David knew what he was talking about when he described being rejected and forsaken by his family. Anyone who has been through similar trauma will find they can identify with the outpourings of heart that some of the Psalms contain. And yet those Psalms do not end negatively: David had developed a relationship with God that filled the gaps, and met his deepest needs. He knew himself to be loved and accepted by God and could write, 'As a father has compassion on his children, so the LORD has compassion on those who fear him' (Psalm 103:13).

God said a similar thing to Isaiah, 'Can a mother forget the baby at her breast and have no compassion on the child she has borne? Though she may forget, I will not forget you!' (Isaiah 49:15). There are many rejected and unloved children around today, who need to know that God can be a Father to them. They will not find out from their own parents. They need to discover it from those who have experienced the Fatherhood of God for themselves, whether single or married.

Enjoying the company of children can help to fill one of the gaps in a single's life. Care is needed not to undermine the parents' authority or to supplant their affection, but we have a lot to offer which can benefit everyone concerned. There are advantages when the children are not our own: we can give them back at the end of a weary day, and go to bed knowing we shall not have to get up if they are sick because they ate too much! We can be selective about what age group we get on with best – I would rather have a bunch of teenagers any day than help in the crèche. Parents have no such choices.

Jesus valued children and his attitude to them shows that they have something to contribute to our lives, whether or not they are our own.

Questions

1. Do I feel comfortable about my own childhood? Are there areas of neglect that I need to allow Jesus to heal?

2. How do I react to children? And how do they react to me? If there are any negatives in these answers, what can I do to change them?

3. How do singles in my church feel about children? Are any of them jealous or bitter – or fed up with babysitting!?

12

Second time single

Quite a high proportion of single people in British churches have previously been married. In the *Singularly Significant* survey they averaged 37 per cent of singles in churches: 4 per cent separated, 9 per cent divorced and 24 per cent widowed. This varied between denominations, with 33 per cent of the Church of England's singles being widows or widowers. In considering singleness from a biblical perspective, this is a group we cannot ignore. Perhaps we can also include here single people who are bereaved after many years of caring for a parent, because they face many of the same emotions and problems.

When I was planning this book I received a letter from another member of my missionary society, whose wife had recently died. He recognized that he was having to face singleness, but wrote, 'One deep truth I am beginning to grasp is an extension of what I have long preached – both singleness and marriage are gifts from our loving Father to be equally enjoyed. Now I see that this is too limited – widow(er)hood is also in that category!'

God cares for widows

The Bible has a lot to say about widows, indeed it is a recurring theme of the Old Testament that the Lord 'defends the cause of the fatherless and the widow' (Deuteronomy 10:18). We saw in chapter 6 that how people cared for the fatherless and widows was frequently used by God as a measure of whether a society was just. Right back in Exodus when the law was first given, God's people were told, 'Do not take advantage of a widow or an orphan. If you do and they cry out to me, I will certainly hear their cry' (Exodus 22:22–23).

In Bible times it was a widow who was likely to be left on her own with no one to protect her or provide for her: she became destitute unless she was cared for by her children. She did not inherit anything from her husband, it all went to the children, or to the nearest male relative, whereas a widower kept his home and continued to receive whatever income he had had previously. There were ways and means available for a man to get justice, but it was a husband's job to ensure that his wife was treated justly. It was for these reasons that the prophets so often spoke about justice for widows.

The law also made provision for widows, as well as aliens and orphans, by allowing them to share the Levites' portion of the tithes (Deuteronomy 14:28–29) and to glean the left-over harvest in the fields, vineyards and olive orchards (24:19–21). It was this law that Ruth took advantage of for herself and her mother-in-law, Naomi, both of whom were widows (Ruth 2).

... and widowers

God made special provision for widows, because they were so vulnerable, but he did not exclude widowers from his cares. When Ezekiel was told that his wife would die, his sense of loss and grief was not overlooked by God. The normal reaction would have been for Ezekiel to lament, weep and shed tears, as well as alter his dress and his behaviour in specific ways (Ezekiel 24:16–17). God did not condemn such actions. Indeed the way in which he told the prophet not to do these things shows that the people would have thought it very odd that Ezekiel did not mourn for his wife. That is why it was a sign which powerfully illustrated God's message to them.

Many look to the church when a family member dies, at least for a funeral service, so help and understanding is available at that stage of bereavement. However, grief is a process and can take its toll for a long time. The church is not always good at providing the long-term support. The individual concerned has to come to terms not only with loss, but also with learning to live as a single person again. As for the biblical command for justice, we ought to ensure that widows and widowers are not discriminated against in matters such as housing, because they are now single again.

Those going through a divorce have similar emotions to contend with but the sense of loss may be compounded by guilt or anger and the pain of seeing a partner in a new relationship. The end of the marriage is marked not by a funeral but often by the divorce court and the parties may need considerable help and advice as they negotiate the legal process involved in custody of children, maintenance money etc. The grieving process is made harder by the reappearance of the 'lost' partner, perhaps on an access visit to children, and can take much longer for the divorced than the bereaved. The last thing the separated or divorced people need is condemnation from church people.

All those who lose a partner, for whatever reason, need support and encouragement to discover, or re-discover, God's grace and love as relevant to their trauma.

God's plans for us

Jesus came to fulfil the law, and he did so in respect of widows, just as he fulfilled other aspects of the law. He showed an awareness of and concern for widows that was unusual in his time. Perhaps it was because his own mother was almost certainly a widow by the time of Jesus' ministry. We do not know when Joseph died nor what that had meant for the family, but Jesus had seen and perhaps even felt for himself the way society in his day treated widows. It is one of the human aspects that Luke, the sensitive, caring doctor, brings out in his gospel.

One of the first people to recognize the identity of the baby Jesus was a widow, Anna. Luke takes the time to tell us that she was very old, having been married for only seven years, and had then been a widow for a very long time. The lovely thing about Anna is that she still had a purpose in life: she had dedicated herself to worshipping God, spending her time in the temple in fasting and praying (Luke 2:36–38). That is why she was there on cue to meet the newborn Christ. God's plans for our lives do not end with the loss of a loved one – any more than they begin the day we get married! After a suitable period of grieving, the second-time single needs to be encouraged to seek the Lord about plans for the future.

The next widow mentioned in Luke is the one who fed Elijah during the famine. When he preached at Nazareth, Jesus used her as an example of the way that 'no prophet is accepted in his home town' (4:24–26). Elijah was specifically sent to a widow, and not even an Israelite one either, although Jesus points out that there must have been many widows in Israel at the time. She had the God-given task of keeping

Elijah alive through the drought and famine (1 Kings 17:9).

Widows provided for

Jesus' most famous encounter with a widow was an echo of another of Elijah's acts, and indeed resulted in the people acknowledging that a great prophet was in their midst. In Luke 7:11–17 we meet 'The Widow of Nain'. As Jesus approached the town his crowd of followers encountered another crowd, going the other way. The mood of the two crowds must have been very different and immediately obvious, because those in the one coming out of the town were on their way to bury a young man. Luke specifically tells us that he was 'the only son of his mother, and she was a widow' (verse 12). It would have been the young man's responsibility to protect and provide for his mother, but now he had died.

Jesus saw all this and realized the implications for the mother, probably more than most in the crowd. His heart went out to her – as I am sure it still does to the bereaved – and he just could not leave her in that situation. Without being asked, he intervened, raised the son back to life and 'gave him back to his mother' (verse 15). In doing so, he not only ministered to the widow's present need, but provided for her future!

In Luke 10:38–42 we find Jesus in the home of Mary, Martha and Lazarus. As we saw in chapter 9, there is a possibility that Martha was a widow. It certainly did not stop her opening her home to Jesus and his disciples. Although patterns of housing are changing, widows and widowers are still the single people most likely to have their own home into which they can welcome others.

Justice

The next widow is the 'persistent' one in the parable in Luke 18:1–8. This woman needed justice against her adversary, but because she was a widow she had to fight for it herself by applying to the local judge. This is a classic example of the difficult situation a widow could find herself in, in a society where normally only men took such action. This woman had courage: she did not accept 'No' as an answer, and persisted in her request for justice. Eventually the judge relented, perhaps out of fear that her continual nagging would get him a bad name. Jesus' explanation of the parable reveals the widow not as a character to be pitied, but as one who represents God's chosen ones (18:7). In contrast to the unjust judge, God responds to the cries of his people, and brings about justice for them. Do we share his concern?

Luke related for us in chapter 20 a series of incidents in which Jesus had something to say about widows. We have already looked at the confrontation with the Sadducees over the unfortunate woman who was widowed seven times, and on all but the last occasion was married to another brother. It was in this context that he made it clear that marriage is not permanent, for there will be no marriage in heaven.

Later in the chapter are recorded some strong words of warning from Jesus about the teachers of the law. Outwardly they were all show, trying to make a good impression by their behaviour and their long prayers. This in itself warranted condemnation, but another of their actions was that 'they devour widow's houses' (verse 47). There are several possible interpretations of this, but the most commonly held one is that Jesus was referring to lawyers whom a husband had appointed in his will to care for his widow's estate. These lawyers were entitled to be paid something for the work they did, but some helped themselves lavishly out of the money entrusted to them, even leaving destitute the people they were supposed to be caring for. Jesus' condemnation is consistent with the recurring biblical theme of justice for widows and others marginalized by society.

This is one of those times when the chapter breaks in the Bible do us a disservice, because as Jesus was talking, he looked up and saw an example of what he was saying. The rich were putting large gifts into the temple treasury, presumably making sure that everyone saw their generosity. Jesus noticed a widow slip in unobtrusively among them and put in two very small coins. He drew the disciples' attention to her, to point out that it was not the amount which mattered, but the woman's attitude. She had 'put in more than all the others', because they gave from their surplus, while she had given all she had. The rich would hardly miss what they had donated, whereas the widow had nothing left and now had to trust God to meet her needs. Jesus clearly did not think her action was either stupid or irresponsible.

The care of widows became an issue early on for the Jerusalem church: the need to make the distribution of food to them more equitable resulted in the appointing of the Seven, including Stephen. It is worth noting that these men had to be 'full of the Spirit and wisdom' (Acts 6:3) – caring for widows was seen as an important ministry of the church. However it was not left only to these men: Dorcas, who was probably single herself, used her gift of sewing to provide robes and other clothing for widows in Joppa. The grief caused by her death suggests she was much loved (Acts 9:36–42). Paul made sure that Timothy knew how to treat the widows in the church he was caring for in Ephesus (1 Timothy 5:3–8), while James took up the Old Testament theme of justice for widows and orphans and brought that requirement into New Testament practice (James 1:27).

Widows and widowers are significant people in our churches, often with many years of Christian life and service behind them. We do them and ourselves a disservice if we allow them to think their lives are of no further use. There is much less about divorce than widowhood in Jesus' life and teaching, but the growing divorce rate means that we shall have more and more such people in our churches. They too need our support and encouragement to apply the principles in this chapter, and they too have much to offer.

Questions

1. *For the bereaved or divorced*: in what ways is God my defender and provider?

2. *For the married*: have I given serious and prayerful (not morbid) thought to the possibility of life on my own if my spouse dies before I do?

3. *For the single*: how can I use my experience as a single person to help someone, who has recently been bereaved or divorced, to come to terms with being single again?

13

Rejection

There is one emotion that is frequently experienced by single people whatever the reason for their singleness, but seems less common amongst the rest of the population. It is rejection.

The divorced are likely to feel it most keenly, especially if their spouse walked out on them for another partner. In 1979 over a thousand couples who divorced were traced to see if they remarried quickly: 34 per cent of men and 33 per cent of women did remarry within three months. The strong implication is that the previous marriage ended because of the desire for the subsequent one. The other partner is almost certain to have experienced some degree of rejection.

An alternative reaction is a sense of betrayal. Those who married as Christians sometimes feel betrayal more strongly because they were conscious of making their vows before God. It is estimated that getting on for half of all marriages taking place in Britain now will eventually end in divorce, with a higher percentage in the USA and some other European countries. It is horrifying to realize how many hurt and rejected people there are and an increasing number of them are to be found among church congregations.

The person who has never been married may feel a less specific kind of rejection: because no one has chosen him or her as a partner, some come to believe they are not worth loving. Lack of a longed-for spouse can feel like the ultimate rejection.

The bereaved frequently have to endure yet another sort of rejection in our society which does not know how to cope with death. It is enormously puzzling and hurtful to be avoided because people do not know what to say or how to relate to you after a partner has died. Part of the process of grieving sometimes involves a sense of having been betrayed or abandoned by the one who has died.

Of all the struggles singles have, enduring rejection is the one that we find most evidence of Jesus having to face too. He was rejected by his home town, misunderstood by his family, persecuted by the religious leaders, abandoned by his followers, betrayed by someone who had lived with him for three years and finally, forsaken by his Father. He knows what it feels like, so he can identify with us in whatever way we feel rejected.

Jesus rejected at Nazareth

The events at Nazareth when Jesus was thrown out of the synagogue were fairly dramatic, according to Luke. There was virtually a riot as they drove Jesus out of the town and tried to throw him off the cliff (Luke 4:28–29). Mark gave us more details about the reactions in Nazareth. Here was someone they thought they knew: 'Isn't this the carpenter? Isn't this Mary's son and the brother of James, Joseph, Judas and Simon? Aren't his sisters here with us?' (Mark 6:3). He had never behaved like this before; where had he got these ideas and powers from? Familiarity breeds contempt: he was acting out of character, and without their permission! The result was tragic for them: 'he could not do any miracles there, except lay his hands on a few sick people and heal them' (verse 5). There was such a lack of faith that it amazed him.

It can be a sad shock the first time we encounter rejection. For some it has unfortunately been a life-long experience which colours all their relationships. But for others it rears its ugly head at a time when they are least prepared for it and most need to be accepted, perhaps after a separation or bereavement.

Whatever Jesus' personal feelings were, about the attitude of the Nazarenes, Luke tells us that he got on with the job. 'He went down to Capernaum, a town in Galilee, and on the Sabbath began to teach the people' (Luke 4:31). The reaction was very different, 'they were amazed at his teaching' (verse 32). Just because one group of people rejects us does not mean that everyone in the world will, although we may feel as though they have! Life itself has not come to an end, there is something worthwhile that we can get on with.

Misunderstood by family

Perhaps the incident at Nazareth had coloured the attitude of Jesus' brothers to him, for when the Feast of Tabernacles approached, they challenged him to go and perform some of his miracles where the world would see him (John 7:2–4). They did not understand who he was or what he was doing any more than their fellow Nazarenes. They 'did not believe in him' either (verse 5), and we do not find a change of heart until after the ascension when they and their mother Mary were in the upper room with the disciples (Acts 1:14).

Persecuted by religious leaders

The outburst at Nazareth happened in the synagogue, and it set a pattern for the reaction of the religious leaders. Some of them had exactly the same objections, 'Is this not Jesus, the son of Joseph, whose father and mother we know? How can he now say, "I came down from heaven"?' (John 6:42). Grumbling at God and his messengers was a characteristic of the Jewish people. It happened time and time again in the wilderness: they grumbled about the water they had to drink (Exodus 15:24), the food God provided (Numbers 11:4–6), their hardships (Numbers 11:1) and just about everything else! Later in their history when they wanted a king, they complained against Samuel. God's assessment of them was, 'it is not you they have rejected, but they have rejected me as their king. As they have done from the day I brought them up out of Egypt until this day, forsaking me and serving other gods, so they are doing to you' (1 Samuel 8:7–8).

The process was repeating itself: Jesus later told the disciples that 'he who hates me hates my Father as well' (John 15:23). He illustrated this in the parable about the landowner who rented out his vineyard. Servants whom he sent to collect the subsequent harvests were treated disgracefully, culminating in the owner's son being killed. The chief priests and Pharisees were furious about this story, because they knew Jesus was talking about them and their rejection of him (Matthew 21:33–46).

People who have been on the receiving end of rejection are in danger of doing the same thing: seeing anything negative that happens to them as a sign that God has rejected them too, and so rejecting him. The Jews did not understand Jesus' message, and their antagonism towards him grew from that time onwards, ultimately resulting in their putting him to death. Rejection of his message led to rejection of him as a person.

Deserted by followers

It was not only the Jews who grumbled about Jesus' teaching at this period of his ministry but many of his own followers did so too. They felt that his teaching demanded too much and responded with, 'This is a hard teaching. Who can accept it?' (John 6:60). The outcome was that 'from this time many of his disciples turned back and no longer followed him' (verse 66). What a contrast to the excitement after the feeding of the five thousand that we read about at the beginning of the chapter!

We could be tempted to think that Jesus would be unaffected by these disciples walking out on him. Far from it. His question to Peter has an uncertainty, a pathos, about it which is surprising: 'You do not want to leave too, do you?' (verse 67). It appears that Jesus genuinely thought they might want to, even though they were the ones he had chosen (verse 70).

Betrayal

They did not leave then, but there came a time when they did. However, even so early in his ministry, Jesus knew that Judas, although one of the Twelve, was going to cause problems later. Judas had other faults, including being a thief who helped himself to the money in the communal purse (John 12:6). Nevertheless he stayed with Jesus right through the three years, through the good and bad times. When Jesus eventually revealed at the Passover Supper that he knew one of them was going to betray him, he 'was troubled in spirit' (John 13:21). He did not find it easy to accept Judas' treachery. He knows what it feels like to be betrayed by someone who has once been trusted, even loved.

A few hours later, Jesus and the disciples, minus Judas, were in the Garden of Gethsemane. He took with him his three closest disciples as he wanted them to 'keep watch' with him (Matthew 26:38). This was perhaps the time when he needed their support more than any other. To his sorrow, he did not get it, and only a few hours later 'all the disciples deserted him and fled' (verse 56). When we are deserted or betrayed, the circumstances are significantly different. Nevertheless Jesus knows what we are going through and can help us.

Forsaken by God

He faced one further step, the ultimate rejection of being forsaken by God. As Jesus took the weight of our sin upon himself, God withdrew his presence because he could not look upon sin (Matthew 27:46). Those who follow Jesus faithfully, will never experience being totally rejected by God. Sometimes it may feel that way, but as the famous story *Footprints* illustrates, God is still there. Jesus said about his sheep, 'I give them eternal life, and they shall never perish; no-one can snatch them out of my hand' (John 10:28).

Acceptance

All human relationships are fallible, and the ultimate healing for rejection is not found at a human level. We discover it when we become convinced that God loves us and accepts us; that when he said 'Never will I leave you, never will I forsake you' (Hebrews 13:5) he meant me!

God accepted Adam before the fall and he accepts us as redeemed individuals. However, God recognized that Adam had a need for human companionship in his observation, 'It is not good for the man to be alone' (Genesis 2:18a). Having recognized the need he then answered it by creating Eve; 'I will make a helper suitable for him' (verse 18b). But there are other ways than a marriage partner for that need to be met.

Being accepted by brothers and sisters in Christ is also a wonderful experience. Paul pleaded with the Christians at Rome to show this attitude (Romans 15:1–7). He reminded them that we should each 'please his neighbour for his good, to build him up' (verse 2). Paul put this in context by reminding his readers that Christ was insulted, but that is not an excuse for us to insult others.

Rather it should encourage us to endure, and give us hope. The prayer in these verses sets a high standard of behaviour for the Romans, and therefore also for us: 'May the God who gives endurance and encouragement give you a spirit of unity among yourselves' (verse 5). This unity is to be expressed in praise toward God and in our attitudes to one another. He pleaded for Christians to 'Accept one another, just as Christ accepted you' (verse 7). It would be thrilling if that happened in all our churches – if everyone, whether single or married, young or old felt accepted. Think what joy and healing that would bring to those who feel rejected!

Questions

1. Do I really believe that God loves me and accepts me? If so, how can I express this to others? If not, what stops me?

2. How can those in my church who have been hurt by rejection experience acceptance in the way Paul encouraged?

14

Love

Do you remember as a child lifting the icing off a piece of cake and keeping it till last, or saving the biggest Christmas present until you had opened all the others? Perhaps you still set aside as a final treat the crunchy bit of the roast potato, or the largest strawberry!

We sometimes keep the best till the end so that we can savour its delights. That is what I have done in this book, because we come now to look at the love of God, demonstrated for us in Jesus. It is expressed wonderfully in John 15, with a summary in verse 9: 'As the Father has loved me, so have I loved you'.

What is love?

The English language does 'love' a disservice because of the multitude of meanings covered by the one word. I can love chocolate and love my family. Songs and poetry frequently use the word to mean the sexual act, while on the other hand adverts tell us how we will love the result if we use their product. Then we read a chapter like 1 Corinthians 13 or John 15 and find that God loves us and he wants us to love him and others!

One of our basic human needs is for love, but of what kind? Our emotions tell us that while we may sometimes crave chocolate, our need is for something much deeper and more permanent.

The variety of words used in New Testament times to describe different aspects of love is well known, but let us remind ourselves briefly what they are:

Agape is used in classical Greek to express the highest and noblest form of love which is directed towards something very precious. In the New Testament it most often describes God's love for his Son Jesus, and for us. It is also used when Jesus tells us to love one another (John 13:34).

Phileo is more tangible, describing intimate affection or pleasant things that we like doing. In Scripture we find it is used about relationships with family and friends (e.g. Matthew 10:37), although it is also used once or twice of God's love for us or ours for him.

Philadelphos is brotherly love for fellow-Christians such as when Peter tells us to 'love as brothers' (1 Peter 3:8).

Eros, another Greek word, means sexual love from which we get our word erotic. However, this word does not appear in the New Testament.

As we have seen, Jesus did not experience the sexual *eros* kind of love but that does not mean he did not show love to people. Far from it! He had an intimate relationship with his Father which he did not keep to himself, for we are told that he loved his disciples. We also know of his love for a few specific individuals such as 'the disciple whom Jesus loved' (John 13:23) and that he 'loved Martha and her sister and Lazarus' (John 11:5). It is quite possible to know what the Bible says about God's love, and yet not ever to have experienced it. It is important for everyone, including singles to discover Jesus' love for them as unique individuals.

Unconditional love demonstrated

Love was one of the themes of Jesus' last few hours with the disciples, which John recorded for us in such detail in chapters 13–17. He did not just teach them about love: he preceded his teaching by washing the disciples' feet, as a demonstration of his love: 'having loved his own who were in the world, he now showed them the full extent of his love' (13:1). This action confirmed that he meant what he said.

His love may sometimes be revealed to us in a spiritual 'touch' on our lives, but it is most frequently demonstrated in a practical way through other Christians. I knew a lady who was a widow and lived a lonely life, with few visitors. She became a Christian in her seventies, and joined a Bible Study group. At Christmas and on her birthday members of the group sent her cards. She was overwhelmed and her whole outlook on life changed as she realized what it meant to be loved.

When Jesus washed the disciples' feet, no one was left out. He included Judas who was about to betray him, as well as Peter who, as he often did, thought he had a better idea! One of the amazing things about God's love is that it is unconditional. We know John 3:16 so well that we can lose the impact of its truth: God loved the world – every person in every generation, in every location. He sent his Son so that 'whoever' believes in him can have eternal life. Age, sex, nationality, marital status are irrelevant as far as God is concerned: he loves us! He doesn't just have a general, vague sort of love that somehow includes everyone, he loves each of us individually and uniquely. He does not ask us to become better people before he loves us because he 'demonstrates his own love for us in this: while we were still sinners, Christ died for us' (Romans 5:8).

Love one another

Jesus' final teaching on love began when he gave his disciples a new command, to 'love one another' (John 13:34). It is one thing to love one's family and friends, most people do that, but being commanded to love one another may have reminded them of Jesus' instruction to 'love your enemies' (Luke 6:27). However, in this last discourse before his death, Jesus was not thinking so much of the outside world, but of his followers.

If we demonstrate the love of God in our relationships with fellow-Christians it has two results. First of all we ourselves learn to live loving lives, to give, and receive, love to a much wider range of people than only our family and friends.

The second outcome is the powerful witness that such love is: 'By this all men will know that you are my disciples, if you love one another' (John 13:35). We do not need to look far in our world today to see there is little love around. In almost every part of the world there are conflicts between ethnic groups, often based on hatreds going back hundreds of years At a personal level, love is undermined by the breakdown of family life, whether through divorce or as young people move to the cities to look for work. In any and every society a community where people have genuine, caring love for one another is a powerful witness to the change the gospel can make.

We can live like this because we do not have to work up this love neither do we 'fall' into it. Christians need love as much as anyone else, but we have a source for it which is not available to others:

'God has poured out his love into our hearts by the Holy Spirit, whom he has given us' (Romans 5:5). This kind of love does not come naturally, but only as we allow the Holy Spirit to control our emotions as well as our thoughts and actions.

It is a cycle of love, triggered by our obedience to God: 'Whoever has my commands and obeys them, he is the one who loves me. He who loves me will be loved by my Father, and I too will love him and show myself to him' (John 14:21). If we love someone, we want to please them, and so it should be with God: we love God so we want to please him and we please him by obeying his commands. In response he shows his love to us which makes us love him all the more and this turns obedience to God from the cold legalism of the Pharisees into a joy.

Fruitful love

Jesus himself found that to obey his Father and to experience his love was a joy: 'If you obey my commands, you will remain in my love, just as I have obeyed my Father's commands and remain in his love. I have told you this so that my joy may be in you and that your joy may be complete' (John 15:10–11). This is a unique privilege for Christians – love and joy like this are not part of the teaching of any other major world religion.

Jesus' thoughts and teaching are never totally centred on the church. Even in John 15, with all its great teaching on love, the intention is not that we should feel happy and secure (though that happens too!), but that we should 'go and bear fruit' (verse 16). One of the anticipated outcomes of a loving marriage is reproduction. So with the church: our loving relationships with God as our Father and Jesus who

119

showed us that love in his death, should result in reproduction.

Another biblical use of the word 'fruit' is to describe the Christian character, the fruit of the Spirit. The first listed is love, and someone has said that all the fruit can be described in terms of love in action in one way or another. As we grow in God's love the fruit of the Spirit grows, so fulfilling God's purpose that we 'be conformed to the likeness of his Son' (Romans 8:29).

This love relationship with our Father also has a bearing on prayer; they are linked twice in these few chapters. Prayer is one aspect of this circle of love: we love God so we want to communicate with him and please him by obeying him – he loves us and delights in our obedience, and one result is 'the Father will give you whatever you ask in my name' (John 15:16; 16:23).

In Jesus' final prayer in John 17, we find yet again the amazing love of God, a love which is meant to be a witness to the world. Jesus prays for 'those who will believe in me through their message' (verse 20), in other words us! Part of his prayer for the church in all places and at all times is for unity 'to let the world know that you sent me and have loved them even as you have loved me' (verse 23). Love is not demonstrated by structures, but by people. Loving unity is seen in relationships rather than through organizational unity.

I have met people who speak a language I do not understand and who have a completely different life style from mine. To be welcomed and loved by them because we are all members of God's family is to experience this unity. Structurally we may have nothing in common, but in terms of relationships there is everything because we are brothers and sisters in Christ.

In his letter to Christians later in the first century, John put the priority of love clearly and succinctly: 'God is love. Whoever lives in love lives in God, and God in him. In this way, love is made complete among us . . . There is no fear in love. But perfect love drives out fear . . . We love because he first loved us . . . Whoever loves God must also love his brother' (1 John 4:16–21).

This is *agape* love. It is not the same as the love between a man and woman. We never come to the end of it: *eros* and *phileo* love are temporary, *agape* love is eternal. Human love grows cold and may die altogether, whereas 'Who shall separate us from the love of Christ?' (Romans 8:35). Paul's resounding answer is all-embracing – nothing whatsoever (8:35-39)!

For the Christian, *eros* love should be directed towards and received from only one person, whereas *agape* love can be given to and received from a wide range of people, as well as God himself. Listening to pop songs, we could be tempted to think that *eros* is the only kind of love there is, but far from it. Discovering and being filled with the *agape* love Jesus offers leaves a much smaller *eros*-shaped gap unfilled, even though we may still at times be aware of that gap!

Questions

1. Have I experienced God's love for me personally? If not, what might be hindering me?

2. Do I and my church live the love of God in such a way that others are drawn to discover God's love for themselves?

15

Leadership

They say we remember very little of what we hear, somewhat more of what we see and perhaps half of what we do; which makes those of us who preach or work in radio think long and hard! The question in any setting has to be how can people see what they hear and then be encouraged to do it for themselves?

Many people do find being single difficult. They may have heard sermons on the subject or read books about it, but to whom do they look for an example of a single person living a fulfilled, fruitful life? The majority of Protestant church leaders are married, although the *Singularly Significant* survey revealed a higher percentage of singles than many suspected – 26 per cent – and more than half the churches surveyed integrated single people into their leadership structures. But what about the other half? Are those singles who are leaders conscious of being an example not only of good leadership but also of fulfilled singleness?

Throughout this book we have looked at the example and teaching of Jesus as a single person. No one questions his ability as a leader. Accepting the general view that Paul was not married, let us briefly look at the kind of example he set, one which single leaders (as well as others) can follow and model. There is a summary of it in 1 Thessalonians 2:6b–12.

Relationships

Leaders need to exercise authority, although how that

happens varies according to the structure of a denomination or organization. Jesus and Paul both demonstrated that authority should not be domineering, but balanced by loving care for individuals (which has nothing to do with whether or not someone has been a father or mother of natural children).

Jesus concerned himself with individuals again and again, while at the same time showing tremendous authority. We often see both in the same event, for example after the incident with the demon-possessed man at Capernaum, 'All the people were amazed and said to each other, "What is this teaching? With authority and power he gives orders to evil spirits and they come out!"' (Luke 4:36). Jesus passed on his authority: when he commanded his followers to 'go and make disciples of all nations', he continued, 'All authority in heaven and on earth has been given to me' (Matthew 28:18–19). Yet he had also commanded them to 'Love each other as I have loved you' (John 15: 12).

The verses in 1 Thessalonians chapter 2 show the same balance in Paul's teaching. He was a brilliant exponent of the Christian faith, but that did not make him aloof and impersonal. He knew the importance of relationships: he saw himself as a mother, brother and father to the Thessalonians: 'we were gentle among you, like a mother caring for her little children' (verse 7); ' . . . you had become so dear to us. Surely you remember, brothers . . .' (verses 8–9); 'you know how we dealt with each of you as a father deals with his own children' (verse 11).

We have looked at these various relationships in previous chapters and seen how important it is, especially for people whose human relationships have been damaged, to discover positive relationships within the church. Paul did not delegate this to others on the basis that he was called to preach and teach. He prayed and wept and pleaded with the Christians for whom he felt responsible, having brought the churches into being.

Paul knew each congregation and taught them truth relevant to their situation. He said to the Thessalonians, 'The Lord's message rang out from you not only in Macedonia and Achaia—your faith in God has become known everywhere' (1:8). His relationship with them was important to him: 'Timothy has just now come to us from you and has brought good news about your faith and love. He has told us that you always have pleasant memories of us and that you long to see us, just as we also long to see you' (3:6). He appealed to them on the basis of those relationships, rather than in a domineering way. He could have demanded much of them because of his status as an apostle, but he did not exercise his authority in that way.

Ministry

In their different ways, both Jesus and Paul were commissioned by God to carry out a specific ministry. Jesus' main purpose was to 'save his people from their sins', as the angel explained to Joseph (Matthew 1:21). Jesus knew that he had come down from heaven to do his Father's will (John 6:38) and nothing could deflect him from that.

Paul's commission was 'to carry my name before the Gentiles' (Acts 9:15). His missionary journeys in Acts reveal him constantly preaching and teaching, usually in places where the gospel had not been heard before. He and his companions had shared the gospel with the Thessalonians even though circumstances were against them: 'we dared to tell you his gospel in spite of strong opposition' (1 Thessalonians 2:2). Once there was a response Paul spent many hours discipling the converts, or as he put it in Thessalonians 'encouraging, comforting and urging you to live lives worthy of God' (2:12).

God has plans for each of us which it is our responsibility to carry out. Teaching and attitudes in churches have often given the impression that singleness is a problem. It is no more of a problem to be single than to be married or a teenager or elderly! All situations of life have their good aspects which we must make the most of, and their pressures which we can overcome with God's help. Singleness itself is not a problem and the more singles there are who underline this by exercising an effective ministry, whatever that may be, the better models there will be for others to follow.

Life style

Throughout this book we have looked at the example Jesus set in his life style. Paul also practised what he preached and was not ashamed of making sure people realized that he did: 'You are witnesses, and so is God, of how holy, righteous and blameless we were among you who believed' (1 Thessalonians 2:10). Christian standards are radically different from those around us, whether in the first century or in our modern world. Whatever society we live in and whatever our situation there will always be pressures and temptations which, if yielded to, would lead us far away from 'holy, righteous and blameless lives'.

Paul was aware how important it was for people to see in practice the spiritual principles he taught, and to put them to work in their own lives. In several of his letters he exhorts his readers along those lines:

> I urge you to imitate me (1 Corinthians 4:16).

> Follow my example, as I follow the example of Christ (1 Corinthians 11:1).

> Join with others in following my example, brothers, and take note of those who live according to the pattern we gave you (Philippians 3:17).

> Whatever you have learned or received or heard from me, or seen in me—put it into practice (Philippians 4:9).

> You became imitators of us and of the Lord (1 Thessalonians 1:6).

Paul did not lay down different standards for the Christians to whom he wrote from those which he himself lived by. It is a struggle for some to put God first, or to maintain biblical standards of sexual behaviour, and these are areas that Satan loves to attack. When leaders do not practise what they preach it can have widespread consequences: the 'fall' of the American tele-evangelists Jimmy Swaggert and Jim Bakker did enormous damage to the cause of the gospel as well as to the Christian use of television in the USA. But the power of the gospel is available to enable us to 'live lives worthy of God' (1 Thessalonians 2:12). In this, as in everything else, leaders are to be 'examples to the flock' (1 Peter 5:3).

Conclusion

Singleness has its problems and at times it may be necessary to 'carry each other's burdens' (Galatians

6:2). However that is not supposed to happen all the time! Each single person can be encouraged and enabled to 'test his own actions. Then he can take pride in himself, without comparing himself to somebody else, for each one should carry his own load' (Galatians 6:4–5).

Jesus said, 'I have come that they may have life, and have it to the full' (John 10:10). He did not add '. . . but only when you get married'! In Britain singles comprise about one-third of the Christian community. The proportion may vary elsewhere, but however few or many single people there are, enabling more of them to live positive, fulfilled lives should have great effects for the kingdom of God.

The resolution made by WEC International's leaders stated: 'When teaching on marriage or relationships is given to the church, teaching on singleness should be included'. Oh that that would be carried out in all churches! Let singleness be included in preaching, modelled in lives and dealt with positively in pastoral situations. Let it be taught and demonstrated to be a viable alternative for marriage, which for some people is God's best.

In this book I have shown that there is a tremendous amount of teaching and example in the Bible that is relevant to singles. It is there in the Psalms and in the lives of the prophets. The teaching of Paul is as applicable to the lives of single people as it is to anyone else. Above all, the Lord Jesus Christ lived a fulfilled life as a single man: he was the supreme single.

Questions

1. How has my attitude to singleness changed while reading this book?

2. What have I learned a) about myself b) about Jesus?

3. How will I make use of this fresh understanding to help others?

A Scripture index is available for this book on request. Write to:

Heather Wraight,
Christian Research,
Vision Building,
4 Footscray Road,
London SE9 2TZ

Please enclose a stamped addressed envelope.